The Campaign of Princeton

1776 - 1777

The Campaign
of Princeton
1776-1777

BY ALFRED HOYT BILL

PRINCETON, NEW JERSEY
PRINCETON UNIVERSITY PRESS

PRINTED IN THE UNITED STATES OF AMERICA
BY PRINCETON UNIVERSITY PRESS
AT PRINCETON, NEW JERSEY

To

Thomas Jefferson Wertenbaker

in grateful remembrance
of many kindnesses

PREFACE

AS the reputation of certain books is so thoroughly established that nobody feels obliged to read them, so there are certain events in history that are relegated to the convenient category of "what every schoolboy knows" and, it might be added, everybody else is willing to take for granted. Washington's descent upon the Hessians at Trenton in the sleety dawn of the day after Christmas in 1776, his skillful strategic retirement thence a week later, and the battle at Princeton the following morning persist more or less vaguely in the memories of most Americans. But of the circumstances of these events—the British conviction that by overrunning New Jersey they had crushed the rebellion, a conviction shared by all but the most resolute of the patriots; the expedients and makeshifts by which Washington contrived to hold together his dilapidated and discouraged forces; the movement by which he so placed his army that by his second retirement from Trenton he regained the initiative which the swollen river and the doubtful support of his troops had cost him—of all these little is known generally and still less is generally understood.

Trenton, or, at best, Trenton-Princeton is the common designation of the campaign. But picturesque and dramatic as the victory of the morning of December 26 was, it could have counted for little more than a brilliant raid had it not been followed by the operations of the next ten days, of which the victory at Princeton was the culmination. It was these that set the smoldering embers of the Revolution flaming afresh throughout the Colonies and drove the enemy from the complacent occupation of almost the whole of New Jersey to precarious and costly concentrations at New Brunswick and South Amboy, where they controlled little more than the ground they stood on. For the rest of the winter, with the mere shadow of an army, Washington at Morristown was able to prohibit a second advance by land upon Philadelphia.

Forgotten is the part played by the Pennsylvania naval squadron on the Delaware and Putnam's troops about Moorestown and Mount Holly, which resulted in the paralysis of a whole Hessian brigade and a crack regiment of Highlanders for seven priceless days. The night march of Cadwalader and Mifflin to a concentration on the battlefield foreshadows the strategy of Napoleon, but it is unknown, except to students of the war; and few have heard of the day-long delaying action which prevented Cornwallis from reaching Trenton in time to accept the battle Washington appeared to have been waiting to offer him, or of the hot fighting, the "second battle of Trenton," that sputtered and sparkled along the Assanpink in the dusk of that evening. It is with the purpose of placing the chief events of the campaign in the frame of these circumstances, without which they cannot be truly appreciated, that this book has been written.

I am indebted to Professor Thomas Jefferson Wertenbaker's "The Battle of Princeton" for his interpretation of the conflicting testimony of eye-witnesses as to the order of march of certain units of Washington's army on the night of January 2 and certain details of the ensuing action. My hearty thanks are given to Dr. Randolph G. Adams and Mr. Colton Storm of the Clements Memorial Library at the University of Michigan, and to the other members of the Library staff, for cordial hospitality and friendly assistance; to Colonel Arthur Poillon of Lawrenceville, New Jersey, Mr. Edward R. Barnsley of Newtown, Pennsylvania, Mr. Edward L. Pierce and Mr. Howard Russell Butler of Princeton, New Jersey, and Mr. Thomas S. Matthews of New York for much valuable information and many useful suggestions. And again I take pleasure in making grateful acknowledgment of the kindness and untiring assistance of the officers and members of the staff of the Princeton University Library.

ALFRED HOYT BILL

Princeton, New Jersey
October 17, 1947

CONTENTS

MAPS

The Campaign of Princeton
1776 - 1777

CHAPTER I

General Washington Gives a Dinner

· O N E ·

FOR those who called themselves patriots in the Independent States of America, the year 1776 had been drawing to a close in unmitigated gloom. Brilliant successes at its beginning—the British compelled to evacuate Boston, Sir Henry Clinton and a British fleet repulsed at Charleston—had been followed by an unbroken series of defeats and disasters. The American forces had been driven out of Canada; Arnold's flotilla had lost its battle on Lake Champlain. Washington's army had barely escaped capture on Long Island. New York had been abandoned, Manhattan Island traversed in a retreat that Washington called "disgraceful and dastardly." Fort Washington had been stormed, Fort Lee given up, the Hudson opened to the enemy as far as the Highlands. The Jerseys had been overrun, and only by the grace of God and the dilatory movements of General Howe had Washington succeeded in placing the Delaware between his army and its pursuers.

From Philadelphia the Continental Congress had departed in haste to the safer refuge of Baltimore, and each day saw increasing numbers of the more prudent citizens filling their carriages with wives and children, loading wagons with the most precious of their belongings, and driving off through the mud and frozen slush to seek asylum in the country. For so soon as the Delaware was frozen—and that was almost sure to happen on one of these late December nights—the British would cross it on the ice, and there would be nothing between them and the city but the half-starved, ragged, and barefoot remnants of what had been called, to distinguish it from other American forces, "the Grand Army." It is small wonder that Robert Morris, one of the Committee of Three that the Congress had left in Philadelphia to keep in close touch with the Commander-in-Chief, wrote to him on the first day of the New Year: "The year 1776 is over. I am heartily glad of it, and hope you nor America will ever be plagued with such another."

At its very end, however, it had brought a sudden gleam of hope, a victory that shone amid the encircling gloom like the first beam of the sunrise of a new and better day. On December 27th Washington had been able to write to the President of the Congress: "I have the pleasure of congratulating you on the success of an enterprise, which I had formed against a detachment of the enemy lying in Trenton, and which was executed yesterday morning." With only twenty-four hundred of his tattered ill-armed soldiers he had recrossed the Delaware and smashed a brigade of Hessian mercenaries who were reputed to be among the finest troops in Europe, killing twenty or thirty of them, mortally wounding their commander and the officer acting as second-in-command, capturing more than half of them, and putting the rest to ignominious flight. Two days later he was entertaining his captives of the higher ranks at dinner at his headquarters.

Those who wished to minimize the exploit—and the British dearly wished to do so—by calling it a mere raid might do so. But its consequences, the prisoners, and the booty belied the imputation of that phrase.

Lord Stirling, writing to Governor Livingston at Washington's request on the day of the dinner, said: "The effect is amazing: the enemy have deserted Borden Town, Black Horse, Burlington, Mount Holly and are fled to South Amboy." At American headquarters in the Widow Harris's house on the west side of the common at Newtown in Bucks County, Pennsylvania, four captured field officers sat at the table of the Commander-in-Chief, while at the Sign of the Red Lion in the village nineteen officers of lower rank dined with Brigadier General Lord Stirling, who had been kindly treated by the Hessian General von Heister when he had been made prisoner at the battle of Long Island.

The guests wore the black coats of the Knyphausen Regiment or the scarlet of the Lossbergs—both excellent organizations—or the dark blue of Rall's, which, though it had been hastily recruited, had behaved with conspicuous gallantry in the assault on Fort Washington. Placed tactfully out of sight doubtless but securely in possession of the victors were the enemy's regimental standards and company guidons. That of the Lossbergs was a white four-foot square with a crown and monogram, an eagle and *Pro Principe et Patria* worked in gold on its silken folds. Another bore on a green field a lion rampant in a gilded circle and the motto, *Nescit Pericula.* Six double fortified brass three-pounders, three ammunition wagons, forty horses, and a thousand muskets were also among the spoil, and snugly lodged in the Newtown Presbyterian church and the Bucks County jail were 888 more prisoners, the rank and file of the three defeated and routed regiments.

In the warm candle-light of the pleasant room Washington listened with grave urbanity to the Hessian officers seated around his table. The hardship, danger, and grinding anxiety of his venture were behind him; his troops, prisoners, and spoil back safe across the river. The Madeira circulated, loosening the tongues of his guests in halting English and copious German poured forth to an interpreter. For war was still the business of gentlemen. It was only thirty years since Fontenoy, where an officer of the English Guards had requested the French King's Guards to fire first. And both parties on this occasion understood what was fitting between gentlemen, though they had been doing their best to kill each other not many hours before.

In the afternoon Washington had received all twenty-three of the captured officers and encouraged them to talk. They were now comfortably quartered in the inns and private houses of the village. But defeat and the first night of their captivity, which had been spent in the ferry house at McKonkey's ferry after some of them had been compelled to wade ashore through breast-deep icy water, had chastened their arrogant Teutonic spirits. Apparently they found their present situation *sehr angenehm* and basked in the condescension of their captor. They were free, especially the younger ones, of their criticisms of the conduct of Colonel Rall, their late commander, making the most of the liberty of speech that their captivity had conferred upon them, and Washington listened to them with a flattering interest equal to their interest in him.

He impressed them as courteous and polite but very cautious and reserved, and since they were probably still rather at a loss to account for the defeat of their fine battalions by his ragged rabble, it is not astonishing that they thought his physiognomy "crafty." Had they been aware of the operation that he was even then considering they might have found it more so.

· T W O ·

ONLY ten days before, Washington had written to his brother John Augustine that "the game" was "pretty nearly up" unless every nerve was strained to create a new army. His men were daily slipping away, and two days before his advance on Trenton he had written to his Adjutant General, Colonel Joseph Reed, that "necessity, dire necessity will, nay, must, justify my attack." For unless he made the venture, desperate though it was, cold, nakedness, disease, and despair would destroy his army, as General Howe was evidently confident that they would do. And on the existence of that army alone depended the American cause.

Until the fall of Fort Washington in mid-November the American Commander-in-Chief had preserved some hopes of winning the campaign. But the loss of that stronghold, which he had attempted to defend only because the Congress had ordered him to do so, had cost him 3000 of his best drilled and best equipped troops, a great many cannon, and quantities of invaluable supplies. He had stood on the ramparts of Fort Lee on the opposite bank of the Hudson and wept tears of helpless rage and pity to see his men bayoneted by some of the very Hessians who were now his prisoners. Four days later the energetic thirty-eight-year-old Cornwallis had crossed the Hudson, climbed the Palisades with 4000 men and heavy guns, and so nearly surprised Major General Nathanael Greene's 2000 at Fort Lee that in their retreat they left behind them thirty-two pieces of artillery, a thousand barrels of flour, many tents, their

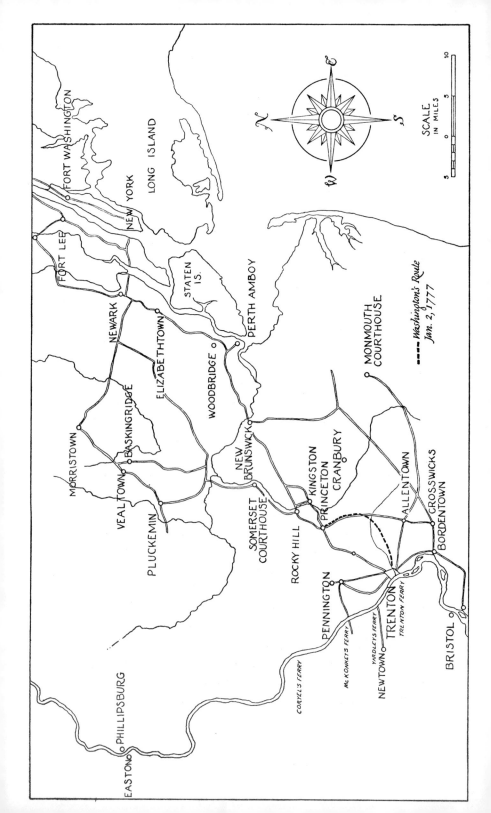

SCALE
IN MILES

FORT WASHINGTON

LONG ISLAND

NEW YORK

FORT LEE

STATEN IS.

PERTH AMBOY

NEWARK

ELIZABETHTOWN

WOODBRIDGE

MORRISTOWN

BASKINGRIDGE

VEALTOWN

NEW BRUNSWICK

SOMERSET COURTHOUSE

PLUCKEMIN

KINGSTON

PRINCETON

CRANBURY

ROCKY HILL

MONMOUTH COURTHOUSE

ALLENTOWN

CROSSWICKS

BORDENTOWN

PENNINGTON

CORYEL'S FERRY

McKONKEY'S FERRY

YARDLEY'S FERRY

TRENTON

TRENTON FERRY

NEWTOWN

BRISTOL

PHILLIPSBURG

EASTON

------ Washington's Route
       Jan. 2, 1777

baggage, and even their blankets. They had reached the bridge over the Hackensack with nothing but their muskets and two twelve-pounders.

Washington, with his actual strength reduced to about 4000 effectives—nearly 5000 of his troops had been made prisoner in the past twelve weeks—could only retreat, and he could do that only with difficulty. He narrowly escaped being trapped between the Hackensack and Passaic Rivers, and the British entered Newark as he was leaving it. At New Brunswick he placed the Raritan between him and his enemy and demolished a portion of the bridge. But Cornwallis was quick to follow, marching twenty miles in one day over the terrible roads of the time and season, though the British infantryman, with full equipment, carried a load of a hundred pounds and on this maneuver the troops had so far outrun their supply train that they had to subsist on nothing but flour.

At New Brunswick, too, the Maryland and New Jersey militia, their terms of service having expired, left for home, with the enemy only two hours march away. The British artillery opened fire across the river, and the American guns answered them in a cannonade that did little damage to either side. But desertion had become epidemic; no fresh troops joined the army from the country roundabout; to attempt to hold the line of the Raritan with those that remained was not to be thought of, and Washington fell back to the Delaware.

Had Howe not sent Cornwallis orders to wait for him and reinforcements before advancing farther it seems impossible that Washington could have escaped destruction. His army now numbered barely 3000, his men lacked shoes and stockings and even shirts. Regiments that still had tents were ordered to burn them to keep them from falling into the hands of the enemy, since there were no wagons to move them, and for the same reason large stocks of supplies had to be abandoned at New Brunswick. To keep from freezing in the bleak December nights the soldiers lay close together on the bare ground with their feet toward their campfires. For want of camp kettles they cooked their scanty rations on their ramrods. But when Howe's conduct of the war was investigated by a committee of the House of Commons some years later, Cornwallis testified that the fatigue of his troops and lack of supplies had prevented him from making a more vigorous pursuit. He knew right well, moreover, that he was not hunting a harmless quarry. Thomas Paine, whose *Common Sense* had sold 120,000 copies in the first three months after its publication and set the revolutionary spirit flaming throughout the country, bore witness to that fact. He rode in this campaign as an aide to General Greene and pointed out afterwards that Washington's men, though defeated, were not beaten, and Paine was not the man to gloss things over. When ordered to stand for a fight, they never failed to obey, and such was Washington's confidence in them that he sent a detachment of them off to Monmouth County to quell a Loyalist insurrection.

Nevertheless, the week that Howe allowed to pass before he joined Cornwallis with reinforcements was a godsend to Washington. He placed Lord Stirling at Princeton with five Virginia regiments and one from Delaware to observe the enemy, and retired with the rest of his army to Trenton, where he caused the banks of the Delaware to be scoured for miles up and down its course until he had secured not only enough boats to ferry his troops across the river but had made sure that not one remained in which the enemy could follow him. He then returned to Princeton and, as Stirling's command fell back on Trenton, accompanied the pioneers of its rear-guard, personally supervising the felling of trees across the road and the destruction of every bridge in order to retard the British pursuit.

On Sunday morning, December 8th, the last of the American troops were ferried across to the Pennsylvania shore, and when the British advance-guard marched into Trenton, with bands playing and colors flying, just a little later, a salvo of grapeshot greeted them from the opposite bank. It seemed, sneered a British officer, as if General Howe had calculated with the greatest accuracy the exact time for his enemy to escape. Cornwallis promptly led a strong force up the river and occupied Pennington—Penny Town to him and to Washington as well—but, search where he would, not one boat could he find. And a search down stream was equally fruitless.

So Washington's army—all that remained of it—was saved at least for the time being. That was the best that could be said for it. "You can form no idea of the perplexity of my situation," he wrote to his brother. "No man, I believe, ever had a greater choice of difficulties, and less means to extricate himself from them." Only a few of his regiments were now two hundred strong. Some were down to between forty and ninety. The 3rd Virginia had 160 enlisted men with the colors, 450 sick, or on extra duty or on furlough. The Delaware regiment reported ninety-two fit, twenty-eight on the sick list. His "little handful," Washington wrote, was "daily decreasing," and he begged the Congress repeatedly for "a respectable army" with long-term enlistments instead of "the destructive, expensive and disorderly mob" that resulted from dependence on the militia.

But militia was better than no army at all, and some sort of army had to be kept in the field while the new regiments were being raised, equipped, and organized. General Greene considered the Pennsylvania militia to be "disaffected," all but the Philadelphia organizations, which could be absolutely relied on, and Washington himself thought their loyalty so doubtful that he proposed to the Committee of Safety that they be disarmed. Nevertheless, he sent General Thomas Mifflin to Philadelphia and through the surrounding country, and General John Armstrong to various likely counties, to rouse them to action. General William Smallwood, whom wounds received at White Plains had rendered unfit for active service, went recruiting in Delaware and Maryland.

At the request of the Congress several of the city organizations had marched to Washington's support even before he entered their state. Commanded by General John Cadwalader, three battalions of "Associators" —citizens who had agreed to "defend with arms, their property, liberty and lives"—Captain Samuel Morris's troop of light horse, and Captain Thomas Forrest's battery, about 1000 men in all, had joined Washington at Trenton along with a regiment composed of Pennsylvania and Maryland Germans and small detachments of the Hunterdon and Middlesex brigades of the militia of New Jersey. Although, as Captain Morris wrote home, the departure of the Congress only a few days after it had resolved that Philadelphia was to be defended "to the utmost extremity" had "struck a damp on ye feelings of many," a state bounty of ten dollars had induced the Pennsylvania troops to promise to remain in the field for six weeks, and each man who reported for duty had been promised a new pair of shoes and stockings. This promise was not kept. But, fresh from their homes, they were well clothed, well armed, and well equipped.

The plight of the regular troops, on the other hand, was only a little less wretched than it had been during the retreat. Posted at the ferries, of which there were nine in all to be guarded, they "crouched in the bushes," as one of them wrote, or behind the ramparts of the small redoubts erected to defend the landings. Later they built shanties, in which, Stirling reported cheerfully, "they lay compact and well covered with boards." They had enough to eat now, for supply wagons came out regularly from Philadelphia to Newtown, where the Commissary and Quartermaster were located. But their want of clothing and especially shoes continued to be deplorable. Advertisements asking for the donation of blankets for the army had been appearing in the newspapers for a month and had aroused the wonder and pity of humane British officers who chanced to see them. Collections of old clothes and shoes were made in Philadelphia and the surrounding towns, and amid Washington's innumerable preoccupations he found time to write an expression of his gratitude for what the Philadelphia people had "charitably contributed."

The Continental uniforms of buff and blue were close to becoming, as their wearers jested, "all buff." The Riflemen's shirts, which were hunting shirts of linen and were worn by most of the soldiers in the field, were filthy and ragged and often the sole covering of bodies infested with vermin. Dr. Benjamin Rush, who was with the army, greatly regretted that the lack of woollen cloth made the use of these garments necessary. Perspiration, mixing with rain, in linen, he noted, caused the deposit of miasmata which was believed to produce fevers. Certainly fevers were prevalent among these troops. So were pneumonia and dysentery. Typhus made its dread appearance, and deserters spread it over the countryside. The condition of the sick and wounded was pitiable. Even in October one surgeon's mate was the sole medical man for five battalions. The supplies of bandages and drugs had long since been lost or exhausted, and the country apothecary shops generally contained nothing more than Ippecacuana, rhubarb, and Globar salts.

Washington was not in the habit of faring much better than his men. During the campaign he and his "family," as he called his aides and secretary, had often slept on the bare ground. His personal servant, he wrote on the first day of this December, was "indecently and almost shamefully naked," and he complained to the Commissary General that he had no kitchen, though his men had provided logs for it, that there was no room for his servants, and that all of them had colds. Such dinners as the one for the Hessian officers must have been a welcome change from a diet which he described as "no better than stinking whisky (and not always that) and a bit of beef without vegetables." And one of his aides wrote: "We never sup."

Soon after crossing into Pennsylvania, however, he established his headquarters at the comfortable farmhouse of Mr. William Keith about four miles north of Newtown. Immediately before him lay his most pressing cause for anxiety, the defense of the river, which by itself might have been sufficiently engrossing. The line which he must strive to hold stretched from Coryell's ferry to the north, where New Hope now stands, to Dunk's ferry a little below Bristol and Burlington, a distance of thirty miles.

The brigades of Stirling, Adam Stephen, Hugh Mercer, and the Frenchman M. A. de Roche de Fermoy were charged with defending it as far as Bordentown. From there to Dunk's ferry the Pennsylvania militia were on guard. But considering the numbers of these troops, watching would be a better word than defending to describe all that could be expected of them, if the British attempted simultaneous crossings at two or more points, as they probably would do. For although no boats had been left on the Jersey side and the enemy had brought no pontoons with them, there were thousands of feet of lumber and several blacksmith shops at Trenton, and some days passed before it became evident that the British army was incapable of a job of boat-building that the versatile American troops would have accomplished easily. After that there remained the threat of a crossing on the ice when the river froze. But all Washington could do to guard against that eventuality was to direct his brigade commanders to be ready to support one another and to select assembly points well back from the river and routes for a retreat to Germantown.

Below Bordentown he had the assistance of the Pennsylvania navy, which has generally received too little credit for its contribution to the success of the campaign that culminated in the battle of Princeton. From Billingsport, where a chevaux-de-frise of submerged iron-pointed timbers blocked the river approach to

Philadelphia, a squadron of row-galleys and gondolas mounting light naval guns patrolled the Delaware as far as Trenton "Falls" under the orders of Commodore Thomas Seymour. They made it extremely difficult for spies in the British service to cross the river in either direction and afforded easy passage for Washington's secret agents. They frequently landed parties of irregular troops, one of which numbered four hundred, who gathered valuable information, searched houses for obstreperous Tories, captured the enemy's couriers, and beat up his outposts. When a report that the British were repairing the bridge on the road to Crosswicks led Washington to fear a crossing to the southward, a galley was vigilantly attentive to the New Jersey bank between Bordentown and Philadelphia.

But the British showed fewer and fewer signs of aggressiveness as the days went by. Cornwallis retired from Pennington to Princeton and soon followed his commander-in-chief back to New York. A Hessian division occupied Trenton and Bordentown: one brigade making itself comfortable with German thoroughness at the former place, while the other, supported by the British 42nd Foot, extended its lines nearly as far as Burlington.

In the Seven Years War, however, German troops had earned the highest reputation for discipline and courage. The Hessians had displayed these qualities to the undoing of the Americans on Long Island and at Fort Washington. John Adams had written of them: "They are masters of rules for guarding themselves in every situation and contingency. The old officers among them are full of resources, wiles, artifices, and stratagems, to deceive, decoy, and over-reach their adversaries." The 42nd was a Scotch Highland regiment, the famous Black Watch. They had fought at Fontenoy, and there must have been not a few of the older men in Washington's army who had seen their dauntless attack at Ticonderoga in the French and Indian War.

There were, moreover, six brigades of Royal troops in the Jerseys. Major General Sir James Grant, Bart. was their commander, with headquarters at New Brunswick, where two battalions made up of volunteers from the three regiments of Foot Guards formed the garrison. Grant had boasted in Parliament in the previous year that he could march from one end of the American continent to the other with five thousand men. Washington knew that the capture of certain of his dispatches had informed the enemy both of his present weakness and of the still further diminution of his force that the end of the year would bring. So he did not cease to expect an offensive against Philadelphia, although, on December 13th, Howe placed his troops in winter quarters by an order that declared the campaign to be at an end.

· T H R E E ·

At the same time the situation in the rear of the American army was the reverse of reassuring. In Philadelphia it was no secret that the Tories only waited for Howe's crossing of the river to rise in arms. They made great capital of an utterly false rumor that Washington intended to burn the city before allowing it to fall into the hands of the British, and the false charge that patriots had been responsible for the fire that had destroyed a large part of New York in September gave color to the story. Several prominent citizens who had been leaders in the movement for Independence had openly gone over to the enemy and joined Howe at Trenton in expectation of his immediate advance on Philadelphia. Shopkeepers had put up their shutters, schools had been closed, their pupils sent home. So great was the exodus of the inhabitants, so deep the dread of those who remained, that Major James Wilkinson, who rode in late one night, found the city "a dark and silent wilderness of houses"; and when young Thomas Rodney marched in, full of patriotic ardor, at the head of a company from Delaware, he was struck by "the horrid appearance" of the place: nobody on the streets and a general look "as if it had been plundered."

Washington, convinced that the loss of Philadelphia, "from whence so many of our resources are drawn," would be "a fatal blow to America," sent Major General Israel Putnam to be its governor. Putnam was fifty-eight years old and in a rather despondent mood about the future of the cause. A young Hessian officer who was presented to him on New Year's Day wrote of him: "This old graybeard may be a good honest man, but nobody but the rebels would have made a general of him." Putnam, however, had been an officer in Rogers's Rangers in the French and Indian War; he had served against Pontiac and as a volunteer at Bunker Hill; and although he had failed as an army commander on Long Island, he knew how to keep Philadelphia quiet. He issued an order denying the rumor that the city would be burned, clamped down a ten-o'clock curfew, and busied himself with the fortification of a line running between the Delaware and the Schuylkill and including the high ground around Germantown.

Washington suggested to the Congress that a young Polish engineer officer, Colonel Thaddeus Kosciuszko, who had recently entered the American service, be placed in charge of the construction of these works. For it proceeded so slowly that a traveler who arrived at Bordentown about this time reported to the Hessian commander there that it would be a year before it was finished. Information from farther afield was equally unsatisfactory. In New York state General George Clinton told the State Convention that his men were departing without leave in large numbers, and Tryon, the Tory governor, gloated over his success in raising battalions of Loyalist volunteers.

Locally, however, things were going somewhat better. Members of the Pennsylvania Committee of Safety were shocked at the small numbers of militia who answered their call from the state at large. But before young Rodney left the city for the front he saw the militia "pouring in." To get and to keep with the colors enough seasoned troops to sustain these well intentioned but not very reliable levies in action was now Washington's most pressing task. He had, indeed, set about it within a week of his arrival in Pennsylvania. For he had never considered giving up the struggle. If he should lose the line of the Delaware, and if Pennsylvania would not support him, he had determined to retire into the mountains with any die-hard remnants of his army that would accompany him. His neck, he is reported to have said, was not fitted for a halter. Actually he had incurred a far more horrible penalty. The punishment for high treason was still the atrocious one of hanging, drawing, and quartering, according to the common law. In that same letter to his brother, in which he mentioned his perplexities, the very next sentence ran: "However, under a full persuasion of the justice of our cause, I cannot entertain an idea, that it will finally sink, though it may remain for some time under a cloud." And he wrote to General Horatio Gates: "If we can draw our forces together, I trust, under the smiles of Providence, we may yet effect an important stroke, or at least prevent General Howe from executing his plans."

He called on General Philip Schuyler, who was in command at Albany, for such troops as he could spare, and Schuyler, whose sector had been relieved from pressure by the retirement of Sir Guy Carleton's forces to Canada in October, promptly started seven battalions on the march for the Delaware. Up in the frigid casemates of ice-bound Fort Ticonderoga, with a garrison that he described as "a handful of naked, sickly, and ill-attended" soldiers, General Anthony Wayne wrote, between the bottles of Burgundy with which he strove to keep the marrow of his bones from freezing, "My heart bleeds for poor Washington." Not so the heart of General Charles Lee. Lee had been under orders to march to the assistance of his commander-in-chief ever since Washington had begun his retreat across New Jersey, but he had remained throughout November at North Castle, five miles above White Plains.

Charles Lee had his own ideas about the conduct of the war, and especially about what he considered his proper part in it. A colonel in the British army at the age of thirty, he had won the friendship of General John Burgoyne by a brilliant exploit in Portugal in the Seven Years War. After that he had held a major general's commission under the King of Poland and had fought against the Turks. Cherishing a grievance against the Tory government in England, he had been an early supporter of the cause of the American Colonies, had

bought a small estate in Virginia, and had sold his services to the Continental Congress for $30,000 and the
rank of major general.

That he had not been made commander-in-chief of all
the Continental forces had filled him with anger and
chagrin, and as Washington's difficulties grew increasingly greater, he did everything in his power to ruin the
man by whom he chose to feel that he had been unjustly
superseded. While Washington was sending him almost
daily calls for assistance, he told all who would listen
to him, and many who would not, that Washington was
unfit to command a sergeant's guard. He had lately
returned from South Carolina and had contrived to
enhance his already greatly swollen reputation as a
professional soldier trained on European battlefields by
appropriating to himself the credit—which really belonged to Moultrie—for the repulse of Clinton's attack
on Charleston.

It was not very difficult to build up a case against
Washington that fall. After all, what did his record
show? In the French and Indian War he had been forced
to surrender at Fort Necessity, and he had covered Braddock's retreat—nothing more. And in this war, after the
British had evacuated Boston, what was there to show
but a dismal series of defeats and retirements: Long
Island, Harlem, White Plains, Fort Washington, Fort
Lee? And now, without one fight, he was racing for the
shelter of the Delaware.

Such men as John Jay and Benjamin Rush were
among those who were impressed by Lee's pretensions.
He succeeded in infecting even Colonel Reed with the
idea that Washington's strategy was timorous and inde-
cisive. That Washington, on learning of his adjutant

general's wavering loyalty, forgave it is only one more of many instances of his magnanimity. Lee wrote of his own actions about this time: "There are times when we must commit treason against the laws of the State, and the present crisis demands this brave, virtuous, kind of treason."

Pretending that Washington's absence had left him in supreme command east of the Hudson, he attempted to take from General William Heath, whom Washington had charged with the defense of the Highland passes, two New England regiments. He succeeded in diverting to his own command four of those battalions from Schuyler, of which Washington stood in such grievous need, and thus brought his own strength up to five thousand men. Washington's increasingly urgent orders to join him in Pennsylvania he called "absolute insanity." To place his troops at the mercy of Washington's incompetent command would, he maintained, be the ruin of the American cause, and he felt quite sure of being made commander-in-chief if Washington were ruined. Not until the tone of Washington's letters carried a faint suggestion that a court-martial might be the consequence of further delay did he finally, on December 2nd, cross the Hudson at Stony Point and start southward.

The presence of Cornwallis on the direct road compelled him to take a circuitous route by way of Morristown, Pittstown, and Easton. But even so he covered only thirty-five miles in the first week of his march, whereas the battalions from Schuyler, poor in health and short of food though they were, had marched a hundred and thirty over no better roads in the same length of time. By December 12th he had got no farther

than Vealtown, about seven miles southwest of Morristown. Leaving his troops there for the night, he took up
comfortable quarters in a house at near-by Basking Ridge
and, by so doing, all unwittingly performed what was
probably his greatest service to the Revolutionary cause
by allowing himself to be captured by the enemy.

Late in the morning of the 13th—for why should he
rise betimes to expedite a movement that he believed to
be utterly misguided?—he was loitering over his famous
letter that began: "*Entre nous*, a certain great man is
damnably deficient . . . ," when a scouting party of His
Majesty's 16th Light Dragoons, the very regiment he
had led so dashingly across the Tagus fourteen years
before, surprised his guard and carried him off in a dress-
ing gown and slippers through the December cold to be
charged with being a deserter from the British army on
the ground that his resignation of his half-pay commission had never been accepted.

"Oh! what a damned sneaking way to be kidnapped,"
wrote Dr. William Shippen, Jr. from the army hospital
at Bethlehem to Richard Henry Lee, who could thank
his stars that he was in no way related to the prisoner.
But Charles Lee's capture was regarded by the patriots
as a calamity. Those who had been brought to despair
by Washington's steady retirement had cherished the
hope that Lee, striking across the mountains with all
the skill and decision of which he boasted himself to be
possessed, would bring defeat and confusion to some
part of the long British line, which now stretched from
Perth Amboy to the Delaware. They waited eagerly for
news of his treatment in captivity. Washington himself
considered his loss a severe blow to the cause and, when
a false rumor spread that he was imprisoned like a com-

mon deserter, sent Howe a stern warning that, if this continued, he would retaliate upon the persons of British officers whom the Americans held prisoner.

General John Sullivan, who succeeded to the command of Lee's troops, led them onward with due diligence. Marching by way of Phillipville, they crossed the Delaware at Easton in a snowstorm and joined Washington on December 20th. Fatigue, exposure, and privation, however, had reduced their numbers to 2000 by this time, and they were described as "much out of sorts and wanting everything." What was called Gates's division, the regiments sent by Schuyler, which arrived under the command of General Benedict Arnold that same day, numbered only five hundred and were in little better case than Sullivan's men. Gates accompanied his troops but, pleading illness, proceeded to Philadelphia. Washington earnestly wished him to take command at Bristol, and wrote: "If you could stay there only two or three days, I should be glad." But Gates went on to Baltimore, where he at once set to work to intrigue with certain members of the Congress against his commander-in-chief.

· F O U R ·

THE new arrivals found Washington showing, as much as he ever permitted himself to do, the effect of the burdens that had fallen upon his shoulders. To Dr. Rush, who came up from Bristol to see him at this time, he appeared to be much depressed and "lamented the ragged and dissolving state of his army in affecting terms." Major Wilkinson, who had observed him to be always grave and thoughtful, noted that he was now "pensive and thoughtful in the extreme."

The immediate pressure of circumstances had, it is true, been somewhat lessened by Howe's order for winter quarters. A large fleet of transports and warships, which had been reported as passing Sandy Hook, and which had led him to fear that Howe had sent Sir Henry Clinton to attack Philadelphia by way of the Delaware Capes and the lower river, turned out to have Rhode Island for its objective. The news that Clinton had taken Newport, with twenty heavy guns in its fortifications, and had landed 6000 men there was certainly disquieting. So was the appearance of a British squadron off New London. But the Revolutionary spirit was strong in New England. From Connecticut the doughty Governor Trumbull wrote that men were flocking to join volunteer organizations that would serve for local defense until new regiments of regulars could be raised.

Washington sent Arnold off at once to take command of them, and with him went young John Trumbull, the Governor's son. John, who was soon to exchange the sword for the paint-brush, had been on the Lake Champlain front the previous summer and had demonstrated to Gates, what the British proved to be only too true in the following July, that Fort Ticonderoga could not be held against an enemy enterprising enough to haul guns up Mount Defiance. But if the young man gave Washington that information, this was not the time to worry about next summer. Until then the winter snows would defend Ticonderoga, whereas something had to be done at once to revive the waning spirit of the country at large and to hold together the army on the Delaware.

The arrival of Gates's and Sullivan's commands had brought Washington's numbers up to about 6000 effectives, counting the militia. But only a very few of the regulars could be persuaded to re-enlist, and only Small-wood's Marylanders and a small part of Rawlings's, Hand's Pennsylvania riflemen, a part of Ward's Connecticut regiment, and the German battalion could be counted on to remain after the end of the year—in all not more than 1500. All of his men, however, could be relied upon to fight to the last day of their terms of service. They were veterans of the whole long, bitterly discouraging campaign. If they were given a chance to fight and were led to victory, they might be induced to stay with the colors until they could be replaced by the new regiments which the states were raising. And Washington had begun to believe that there was a good chance of giving them both the fight and the victory.

He had an active and excellent secret service, and on it he spent his little hoard of hard money, which he was able to come by only with increasing difficulty. Distrust of the Continental currency had by this time become so general that in Philadelphia £300 of it was offered for £150 of the Pennsylvania state issue, £250 for £150 sterling: and tavern keepers, who dared not refuse it when it was proffered by soldiers, had taken down their signs and declared that they had gone out of business. Only lately Robert Morris had been compelled to levy on himself and several patriotic friends in order to send to the Commander-in-Chief "four hundred and ten Spanish dollars, two crowns, ten shillings and sixpence in English coin, and a French half crown."

One of the ablest of Washington's spies was John Honeyman, who covered his tracks so thoroughly that he was known to his neighbors as a Tory spy and only evaded court-martial by Washington's connivance in his escape, when American scouts brought him in at

American headquarters as a prisoner. He reported that the dispositions of the Hessians across the river were such that the garrison at Trenton might be attacked successfully, and information from other sources confirmed this intelligence.

"Now is the time to clip their wings, while they are so spread," was Washington's comment. But his opinion that the attempt was a desperate one was understood later by Dr. Rush, when he recalled an incident in his visit to headquarters that week. For, as the two men sat talking together, Washington kept scribbling on scraps of paper, and on one of these, which fell to the floor, the Doctor read, "Victory or Death," which was the American watchword at Trenton a few days afterward.

On Monday, the 23rd, orders were sent up and down the river for the troops to prepare and keep on hand three days' cooked rations. That night in a blinding snowstorm Seymour's galleys and gondolas moved up the river as far as Bordentown. The following evening Washington rode over to General Greene's headquarters, the other generals assembled there in a final council of war, and the details of the operation were decided upon. Orders were sent to Cadwalader down at Bristol to cross the Delaware on Christmas night with his Associators and a New England brigade and keep the enemy troops in the Bordentown neighborhood too busy to interfere with the main attack. At the same time General James Ewing, with about a thousand Pennsylvania and New Jersey militia, was to cross opposite Trenton, seize the bridge over the Assanpink at the lower end of the town, and thus cut off the retreat of the Hessians in that direction, while Washington led a picked force of 2400 men and 18 guns against them by way of Mc-

Konkey's ferry and the eastern bank of the Delaware.

In the early afternoon of Christmas Day the troops who were to march under Washington's immediate command were paraded behind a convenient ridge that shielded them from observation from the farther bank. They had their blankets and cooked rations, fresh flints for their muskets, and forty rounds of ammunition, which was a large allowance for battle in any army in those days. But they had little else. The shoes of most of them were broken; some had bound old rags around their feet; many were barefoot; and an officer who was late at the rendezvous found it easily by following their bloody foot-tracks in the light snow that covered fields and hillsides.

If they were short of material things, however, they had a full and rich complement of indoctrination. At the bleak and bitter bivouacs of the retreat Thomas Paine had been writing busily. As soon as he was within reach of Philadelphia his manuscript went to the printers. It appeared in pamphlet form on December 23rd. Copies of it were rushed out to the army. Washington caused it to be read to every corporal's guard, and his soldiers charged down the streets of Trenton two days later, yelling like a crowd of undergraduates, "This is the time to try men's souls!"

As soon as the early winter darkness fell, the boats, which had been hidden behind wooded Malta Island since the retreat, and whose numbers had been augmented in the past few days by a search along the upper Delaware and Lehigh Rivers, were brought down to the ferry landing. The best of them were the Durham boats, which had been devised to carry iron ore and freight between Philadelphia and the northern counties of New Jersey. Ranging from forty to sixty feet in length and eight feet wide, they drew only twenty inches when fully loaded. The largest of them could carry fifteen tons and were capable of transporting the whole of some of Washington's little regiments in a single trip. They had heavy steering sweeps that could be fitted at either end and were equipped with two masts and sails and with poles to drive them against contrary winds and currents.

This night they were handled by Colonel Glover's regiment, those sturdy fishermen from Marblehead whom the British government had deprived of their livelihood by prohibiting Americans from fishing off the Grand Banks. They were armed with rifles, and it was they, in their loose short trousers and blue round jackets with large leather buttons, who had spirited the beaten army away from Long Island in the morning fog at the end of August. But here the river was fiercely swift and filled with floating ice, and although young Knox, with stentorian voice, dominated the embarkation and personally supervised the loading of the artillery, the work was maddeningly slow. Washington had set "Christmas Day at night, one hour before day" as the time for the attack. But as the precious minutes slipped past, it became more and more evident that Trenton could not be reached before dawn, when the Hessians, instead of being snugly in their beds, would probably be astir.

CHAPTER II

Fröhliche Weihnachten!—
Der Feind! Der Feind! Heraus! Heraus!

· O N E ·

THE situation of the Hessians at Trenton and in the Bordentown neighborhood between December 10th and 25th had not been by any means so happy as it must have appeared to the wistful gaze of the American soldiers on the opposite bank of the river. It had grown increasingly worse from day to day, though it had seemed promising enough at first. For the Jerseys had been less unwilling than many of the other states to listen to the proposals for reconciliation put forth by General Howe and his brother the Admiral.

When, in September, those two had joined in proclaiming that the King was "most graciously disposed to direct a revision of such of his Royal Instructions as may be construed to lay an improper Restraint upon the Freedom of Legislation in any of his Colonies, and to concur in the revisal of all Acts by which His Subjects may think themselves agrieved," there were many between the Hudson and the Delaware who were favorably impressed. As Washington fell back slowly across the state, few took up arms to join him in the defense of their homes and firesides, and he said in his haste that the conduct of New Jersey was "infamous." With the help that he had the right to expect, he believed that he could have made a stand at New Brunswick, or even at Hackensack, as he had intended to do.

On November 30th the Howe brothers proclaimed that, whereas "several Bodies of armed Men . . . do still continue their opposition," a full pardon, with the assurance of liberty and the enjoyment of their property, would be granted to all who, within sixty days, would swear to "remain in a peaceable Obedience to His Majesty and not take up arms, nor encourage Others to take up arms, in Opposition to His Authority." Hundreds of people—especially those who had the most to lose, it was observed, and those who had the least to defend—flocked to sign this oath, which could be administered by any British officer.

In return they received a "protection paper." But, unfortunately, the discipline of the British army proved unequal to the benevolent intentions of its commander. Its regiments had been hurriedly expanded for the war by the addition of new companies or by increasing the numbers of companies already in existence. The war was so unpopular in England that recruiting was difficult, and the ranks had been filled with the sweepings of the slums and the scum of the jails. Line officers were lacking: frequently there were but two to a company. These found it impossible to keep their men under control and frankly admitted the consequences, which they deplored.

The promised enjoyment of liberty and security of property by those who took the oath proved to be mythical. Their "protection papers" were laughed at by the British soldiery, ignored by the Hessians, for whom, of course, they might just as well have been written in Greek. Brought up in the traditions of Continental warfare, in which plunder and rapine were accepted practices, King George's Teutonic auxiliaries had been told, moreover, that their service in America would give them the opportunity to found their private fortunes. Their mouths watered at the sight of the good living they observed among people whom they could only classify as peasants, and they behaved accordingly. The goods, chattels, and livestock of those who had renewed their allegiance to the King were taken as lawlessly, their houses, barns, and stables were sacked and looted as ruthlessly, as those of persistent rebels.

Even in friendly New York, where it should have been comparatively easy to enforce the will of the commander-in-chief, soldiers and camp followers looted the public libraries—including the one in the City Hall itself —and 60,000 volumes went into a black market for little more than the price of a noggin of gin apiece. A Tory judge remembered in the bitterness of exile long after, that loyalists were treated no better than rebel sympathizers. Of the campaign in general a British officer wrote that indiscriminate plundering had become "a business . . . a perfect trade," that not even receipts were given for what was taken, and that families were insulted, stripped of furniture and bedding and even of their clothes. The rebels, on the other hand, he observed, wisely permitted their troops to plunder only those who sided against them.

Upon New Jersey, as a British writer of the present day confesses, the invaders "fell tooth and claw." The British soldiery pillaged Elizabeth Town and other places, while their doxies stood guard over the accumulating spoil. From Princeton the leading patriots wisely took flight in time to escape capture: Mrs. Jonathan Sergeant in a wintry midnight; Dr. John Witherspoon, the President of the college and a signer of the Declaration of Independence, riding his sorrel mare at the side of the "old family chair" that conveyed his wife. Their houses suffered for them. Witherspoon's "Tusculum" was stripped of its library of rare books that had come from the printing-houses of Leipzig and Birmingham; its collection of valuable antiquities was scattered or destroyed. Lovely Morven, the home of Richard Stockton, who also had signed the Declaration of Independence and was already a prisoner of the British, was looted of its library and furniture.

Camp women and their bullies pillaged Nassau Hall. Its library and museum, its scientific and mathematical instruments, and the "celebrated orrery," a planetarium that was said to be the finest in the world, went the way of the treasures of Tusculum. Sergeant's fine new house, which stood on the present site of the Nassau Club, was burned. But this was probably by accident rather than design, for the invading troops were desperately in need of housing, and the weather was bitter cold. Nassau Hall and the Presbyterian Church became barracks. Officers and men were billeted without regard to the convenience or comfort of householders.

Some of the depredations, to be sure—the taking of fences and outhouses, boards from buildings and carpenters' stocks of lumber for firewood, and the cutting down of orchard trees for the same purpose—are to be ascribed less to malevolence than to the necessities of soldiers whose requirements were not properly attended to. But the local tannery was sacked: every bit of leather, tanned or untanned, was stolen. Grist mills and a fulling mill near by were burned wantonly together with their contents. Milch cows were stolen at night and slaughtered along with other cattle. And although

Howe had issued stringent orders against pillage, it was believed at Princeton that Cornwallis, General Grant, and General Leslie had stood by while horses and hogs were driven off without any compensation being made for them.

A detachment of dragoons did pay twenty shillings for damage that amounted to £50. But generally no money, at most only a receipt, was given on even the most formal requisition. Informers who supplied the British headquarters with the names of men serving in the American army grew rich with the goods confiscated as a result of their talebearing. But so promiscuous was the plundering that many suspected that the "protection papers" had been issued only to make sure that those who held them would keep their property at hand and so within easy reach of the spoilers. Worse still, the ugly word, rape, began to be whispered about. At Penn's Neck a farm girl was strangled and ravished by two British light horsemen; an outraged father was killed when he shot an officer who attempted to violate his daughter; and several women and girls were suspected of suffering in silence rather than incur the shame incident to bringing accusations against soldiers who had assaulted them.

The thriving villages of Maidenhead (the present Lawrenceville) and Hopewell were described as "broken up," livestock driven off, and hardly a soldier who did not lead away a horse laden with clothing and household linen. It was maintained by the British that their men took only such things as they might have use for, whereas the Hessians were systematic in their pillaging, making lists of their loot, loading their wagons with it, destroying what they could not carry away, and leaving women and children naked and shelterless in houses with smashed windows and broken doors. But Washington appears to have gathered from the reports that reached him that the behavior of the Hessians was less abominable than that of the British.

The natural consequence of all this was that the Jersey people were soon bitterly regretful of their collaboration with the invaders, and they were not slow to take up arms in reprisal for their injuries wherever and whenever it was possible for them to do so.

· T W O ·

THE Hessians at Trenton and in the Bordentown country were particularly exposed to the rapidly increasing hostility of the population. Not only were they at the far end of the chain of posts which Howe had stretched—with "rather too large links," as he himself confessed—from New Bridge and Hackensack to the Delaware in order to secure his conquests, but the Hessian division was itself dispersed beyond the bounds of safety. Its commander, Colonel von Donop, who does not appear to have shared in the contempt for their adversaries that was felt by most of the German officers, had wished to concentrate his force at Trenton. But Howe directed him to occupy Bordentown also and, in order to protect the loyalists in Monmouth County, Burlington as well.

He had trouble from the beginning. Irregulars delayed his march from Trenton to Bordentown by destroying the bridges, and riflemen on the farther bank of the Delaware harassed his column with a fire to which the smooth-bore muskets of his troops could make no effective reply. When he reached Burlington, he was informed by Mayor Lawrence, father of the Lawrence of the *Chesapeake-Shannon* fight in the War of 1812, that if the Hessians occupied the town, Commodore Seymour would bombard it from the river. Seymour threw a few round-shot into the place, and Donop, mindful that many of the inhabitants were loyalists, withdrew. He stationed the 42nd Foot, with one of his grenadier battalions, at Black Horse (now Columbus) until the expected arrival of heavy artillery should enable him to deal with the American flotilla. With the rest of his command—two battalions of grenadiers, a company of Hessian jägers, six three-pounders manned by Hessian artillerymen, and a company of British artillery with two six-pounders and two three-pounders —he himself went into winter quarters at Bordentown.

His situation there was far from satisfactory. Quarters in the village were so inadequate that he had to disperse his men by eights, tens, and fifteens among the poorly built farmhouses of the neighborhood, where they slept in straw on the floors. Otherwise, he reported, they would have perished with the cold, for the inhabitants had fled, taking their bedding with them. He had difficulty in communicating with Grant's headquarters, since he knew little English, wrote to the General in French, and was dependent on the colonel of the 42nd to translate Grant's replies. From Colonel Rall in command of the post six miles up the river at Trenton came a steady stream of reports of annoying guerrilla activity in that neighborhood, and the most contradictory intelligence reached Donop from Pennsylvania. One day he would hear that the American army was sure to melt away at the year's end, the next that Washington had crossed the river above Trenton and was about to threaten Rall's right flank.

On December 16th, only two days after Donop had made his dispositions, he was informed that a party of 300 mounted rebels had been behind him, pillaging the loyalists whom the presence of his troops was supposed to protect and that these marauders had marched to Mount Holly and Moorestown to join General Putnam, whom Donop believed to be at Cooper's Creek with 3000-4000 men engaged in transporting supplies. Donop ordered out patrols on the roads from Black Horse to Burlington and Moorestown and sent a reconnoitering party of 200 foot and a few mounted jägers toward Mount Holly. The enemy's reported 4000 turned out to be only 500, but he decided against attacking them. The bridges had been destroyed, and the circuitous march over swampy roads would subject his troops to fatigue that he considered unnecessary. On the 22nd, however, on hearing that the Americans were at Mount Holly, he rode to Black Horse. A skirmish that afternoon and another the next day lured him into occupying Mount Holly with the 42nd and his Hessian battalion from Black Horse and thus to disperse his command still farther, which was exactly what Washington must have hoped that he would do. The American force had orders to retire as he advanced.

At Trenton the garrison was more comfortable. Trenton was a pretty village. Its location at the head of navigation on the Delaware and at the junction of several main highways had given it considerable importance and prosperity. Its hundred houses, two churches and Quaker Meeting House, and the barracks which had been erected during the French and Indian War enabled Colonel Johann Gottlieb Rall to quarter his whole brigade there instead of scattering it as Donop had been compelled to do at Bordentown. In addition to his three Hessian regiments, which included seven grenadier companies, ten of fusiliers, and six field guns manned by Hessian artillerymen, Rall had fifty Hessian jägers, who were armed with short rifles, and twenty troopers of the British 16th Light Dragoons for messenger service and scouting: about 1400 men in all. But he seems to have regarded his situation with a curious mixture of overconfidence and nervousness.

Rall was, in fact, singularly unfitted for the command at Trenton. Howe had given it to him unwillingly and only because Rall had earned a certain right to insist upon it by his excellent work at White Plains and elsewhere. A veteran of the Seven Years War, he had since served in Russia under Alexis Orloff, the murderer of Czar Peter III. But he appears to have been a mere battlefield soldier. Whereas Donop had some conception of what the Americans were fighting for, and consequently a healthy respect for such military ability as they possessed, Rall had the military aristocrat's contempt for the raw troops he had three times defeated, for the artillery, mostly iron guns on naval carriages, which his men had captured on Long Island, and for the lawyers, farmers, shopkeepers, and blacksmiths who pretended to be generals. For Howe's policy of reconciliation he was worthless, and his ignorance of the English language handicapped seriously his service of security and intelligence.

He placed strong and vigilant outposts on all the roads leading to the village, at the ferry landing below the mouth of the Assanpink, and at the drawbridge at the mouth of Crosswicks Creek on the road that connected him with Donop's headquarters at Bordentown. He provided for diligent and frequent patrolling of the roads by dragoons and jägers. In fine weather arms were stacked under guard in front of the quarters of his regiments. One regiment was kept always under arms, its men allowed to take off only their gaiters when not actually on duty.

When his outposts were beaten up, his patrols attacked, and his messengers to Princeton killed or captured by local guerrillas or scouting parties from across the river, as they were with ever increasing frequency, the notes in which he informed Donop of these occurrences had a nervous undertone hardly to be expected of an officer of his experience. He urged upon Grant at New Brunswick and upon Leslie at Princeton the necessity of placing the wing of a regiment at Maidenhead lest his communications be cut entirely. When Grant refused, with the comment that he could keep the peace in New Jersey with a corporal's guard, Rall sent a hundred men and a cannon to escort his next messenger.

On the other hand, instead of placing his guns in positions where they would be of immediate service in the event of an attack, he had them parked, first, in the graveyard back of the English church and, later, one behind another in the middle of King Street in front of the building that was used as a guard-house. He neglected to build a redoubt at the top of the village, where the roads from Pennington and Princeton made a junction with the heads of King and Queen Streets (now Warren and Broad Streets), the principal north and south thoroughfares, although Donop had given him orders to do so and sent an engineer officer to design the work.

He indulged himself in a life of amusement and a degree of comfort that, in the circumstances, amounted to luxury. One of his officers said that he never visited an outpost. After nights spent at cards and drinking he slept late, but he kept his command, officers and men alike, weary and disgruntled by a daily program of drills, ceremonies, and useless patrols. Each day the guard, with the band at its head, must march around and around the churchyard "like a Catholic procession," a Hessian officer wrote, "lacking only the banner and the chanting choristers." The troops returning from parade must pass under his windows, and if he had not yet finished his bath, though it might be ten o'clock in the morning, they had to be kept waiting in the cold until he was ready to look at them.

He delighted in the mechanical perfection of their drill, in their coats of red, blue, or black, or the green of the jägers; in their yellow waistcoats and breeches and long black gaiters, their broad cross-belts that supported cartridge-pouches, bayonets, and brass-hilted swords; in their fierce mustaches blackened with shoe-blacking, and the tall brass-plated caps that crowned heads dressed with a mixture of tallow and flour. But he was as indifferent to their health and comfort as he was to a thorough provision against attack, and consequently many of them fell sick.

When his regimental commanders went to him with a request that he send to New York for a supply of warmer underclothing for their men, who were suffering from the cold, they met with a jocular refusal. As the days went by and Trenton became almost a village beleaguered, so frequent grew the attacks on outposts and patrols, all of his officers felt an increasing concern over the vulnerability of their situation. But when Major von Dechow of the Knyphausen Regiment, who had been one of Frederick the Great's old officers, went to Rall and urged him to build the fortifications that had been ordered, Rall's reply was: "Let them come. We want no trenches. We will go at them with the bayonet."

A Tory farmer from across the river brought him warning that Washington was about to move against him. A couple of deserters told him of the preparation of cooked rations by the American troops, and on the 23rd Doctor William Bryant of Bloomsbury Farm corroborated their report. But Rall replied impatiently: "This is all idle. It is old woman's talk." When he fell fighting with bull-headed tenacity and stupidity three days later, no tears were shed for him. An English contemporary summed him up as "noisy, but not sullen, unacquainted with the language, and a drunkard." One of his lieutenants, still smarting from the defeat for which he held his commander solely responsible, composed this epitaph:

> *Hier liegt der Oberst Rall,*
> *Mit ihm ist alles all.*

On the 24th, however, when he heard from Grant that "a good line of intelligence" indicated that the Trenton garrison would do well to be on the alert, Rall mounted his horse and, with twenty of the British dragoons, accompanied one of two patrols, each a hundred strong, which he sent up to Pennington, one by the River road and the other by the direct route. They chased a party of some thirty Americans back to their boats at Johnson's Ferry, wounded three of them, and drew the fire of the American battery on the farther bank. That was all, and Rall flouted his officers' suggestions that it might be prudent to move the baggage— i.e. the plunder—to a place of greater safety.

Next morning, Christmas Day, he appears to have heard from Grant that Lord Stirling had been reported in the neighborhood with a small detachment. But all he did was to ride about the outskirts of the village that afternoon and visit some of the guards. Between seven and eight o'clock he was enjoying a game of checkers at his headquarters on King Street with his host, Mr. Stacy Potts, when a volley of musketry, followed by a few scattering shots, broke the frosty stillness of the winter evening.

The happenings of the next several minutes ought to have impressed him with the inadequacy of his arrangements, but they did not. No alarm stations had been designated, and the result was turmoil and confusion. Rall, at the head of his own regiment, which was the regiment *du jour* and so under arms that day, marched to the high ground where the Pennington and Princeton roads entered the village. The Lossbergs and Knyphausens assembled in front of their quarters, where their commanding officers were compelled to leave them and go in search of the brigade commander for orders.

It appeared that forty or fifty of the enemy had attacked the outpost on the Pennington road, wounding six of the sixteen soldiers of the Lossberg regiment who held it, and had then retired in the direction of Johnson's Ferry. A patrol that went two miles up the Pennington road failed to find any traces of them, and the troops were ordered back to their quarters. Major von Dechow urged that strong patrols be sent out along all the roads and to all the ferries. But Rall replied that the morning would be soon enough for that. The enemy, he believed, were probably only a party of farmers, which he could handle with his regiment alone.

Dechow, still apprehensive of an attack, ordered his men to remain indoors, ready for action. But Rall, who had been given a second chance, if ever a man had, cast care aside, confident that he had taken the true measure of the enemy's offensive. He dropped in at Mr. Abraham Hunt's at King and Second Streets for a jovial supper. Afterwards the cards were running so well that he put into his pocket unread a final note of warning that a Pennsylvania farmer had scribbled at the door on being refused admittance by the Negro butler. The wine was so excellent and his host so bountiful that it was long after midnight when Rall got to bed, and he was evidently quite drunk.

Like master, like man. Modern doubt has assailed the legend of the Hessians' drunken orgy this Christmas night. It is true that the British commissaries had been able to obtain so little beer for the troops that they had supplied spruce beer instead; true also that Madeira cost three shillings and sixpence a bottle at Trenton, a fearful price for frugal German officers. But judging by the supplies that Washington captured next day, there was plenty of rum for everybody to drink *"Fröhliche Weihnachten,"* and in the grim dawn a few hours later many an aching head must have been jarred by the musket shots and the shout of *"Der Feind! Der Feind! Heraus! Heraus!"* that rang out above the

moaning of the wind and the steady beating of the
sleet against the windowpanes.

· T H R E E ·

H AD Rall listened to Dechow's urgings and sent
strong patrols up the Delaware that evening they
would doubtless have encountered the first of Washington's troops already on the Jersey shore, and the campaign that changed the history of the world might have
ended where it began. For Stephen's brigade of Virginia Continentals was over the river not long after
seven.

They immediately threw a chain of sentinels around
the landing place. Washington followed them, with his
lieutenants, and sat down, silent and imperturbable, on
a box that had once been used as a beehive, to await the
debarkation of the guns and the rest of his little army.
Few men knew better than Washington how to endure
the torment of uncertainty. He had done everything in
his power to ensure the success of his enterprise. Every
officer had been ordered to wear a piece of white paper
in his hat to distinguish him in the darkness; every
officer's watch had been set by that of the commander-
in-chief; Doctor Shippen and his aids had been directed
to come down from the hospital at Bethlehem to take
care of the wounded, who seemed likely to be numerous.

The swirling river and the grinding ice cakes in ever
increasing numbers threatened to smash the heavily
laden boats in spite of all the skill and strength of the
men from Marblehead. The cold was intense: "as severe
a night as ever I saw," young Thomas Rodney wrote of
it. And to crown all a storm of rain, hail, and snow
swept down upon the river, driven by a fierce northeast

[44]

wind. The men of Moulder's battery, longshoremen, shipwrights, ship's carpenters, and the like from the Philadelphia waterside gave expert help to Glover's men. The Hopewell township people, burning to avenge the insults, depredations, and ill treatment they and their families had suffered at the hands of the British and Hessians, turned out to help the debarkation and lent a hand at hauling the boats through the icy shallows. But it was after three in the morning, instead of midnight as had been anticipated, when finally the advance began.

Sullivan led the right wing, which was made up of New Hampshire, Massachusetts, Connecticut, and New York men picked from the brigades of St. Clair, Glover, and Sargent. Greene commanded the left and had under him Stephen's Virginians; Mercer's brigade, which was composed chiefly of Continentals from Connecticut, Maryland, and Massachusetts; Haslet's brigade, made up of the Delaware regiment, two regiments of Pennsylvania Continentals, and a Pennsylvania rifle regiment; and a brigade composed of another Pennsylvania regiment and a regiment of Germans from Pennsylvania and Maryland, which was commanded by de Fermoy. Four batteries of artillery marched with the right wing; three, and Captain Morris's Philadelphia troop of light horse, with the left. In all there were eighteen of those precious guns which the army had brought through the retreat across New Jersey without losing one of them.

"Shoulder your firelocks," came the order, and the troops took the road inland in single column for the first four miles, which brought them to the little hamlet of Birmingham. There they ate a hasty meal out of

their haversacks, while Washington, without quitting
the saddle of his chestnut sorrel charger, partook of some
food sent out to him from the house of Mr. Benjamin
Moore.

It was bitter hard marching, even for the men with
shoes, on the slippery rutted surface of the half-frozen
road. When the order to resume the advance was given,
a good many men had to be wakened from sleep in the
slush and snow of the roadside. The delay and the
dreadful weather had made all the officers "gloomy and
despondent," as Major Wilkinson remembered that
night. But Washington in his report to the President of
Congress next day wrote of both officers and men: "The
difficulty of passing the river in a very severe night, and
their march through a violent storm of snow and hail,
did not in the least abate their ardor." He had reason to
feel the highest confidence in them. They had been
chosen, for the most part, from the hard-bitten remnants of the regiments that followed him from the Hudson, and their officers, from the generals down, had
been repeatedly tested in action.

Colonel Henry Knox, the twenty-six-year-old Boston
bookseller, had fought at Bunker Hill; during the previous winter he had brought the guns from captured Ticonderoga through the snowy defiles of the Berkshires
to the siege of Boston; and he was by way of becoming
a consummate chief of artillery. After the stunning defeat of Long Island he had written his wife: "One or
two drubbings will be of service to us; and one defeat
to the enemy, ruin." Since then the drubbings had been
far more than one or two, and the defeat of the enemy
was still to be accomplished, but he was as confident as
ever of its effect.

Of the commanders of the two wings of the army, Major General Nathanael Greene, Rhode Islander by birth, thirty-four years old, and a blacksmith by trade, had always kept a book beside him as he worked at his forge, and had earned the name of "the learned blacksmith." Before this war was over he had demonstrated a "native genius" for generalship and was considered by Cornwallis to be "as dangerous as Washington." In marked contrast to Greene was Major General John Sullivan. Born in what is now the state of Maine and two years older than Greene, Sullivan had become a wealthy New Hampshire lawyer. He was an excellent officer, and it had been no fault of his that at the battle of Long Island he and his command had been assailed in front and rear and had been made prisoners.

Four of the brigadier generals were veterans of the French and Indian War. They ranged in age from Hugh Mercer, who was fifty-one, to Arthur St. Clair, who was forty. Born in Scotland, Mercer had left medical school in his fourth year to join Prince Charlie's army in 1745, had dressed wounds with sour wine and moss at Prestonpans, and fled to America, a hunted fugitive, after Culloden. He had had an adventurous career as captain and major of Pennsylvania troops in the French and Indian War and had distinguished himself by bringing the garrison of Fort Pitt through its terrible first winter. Later, through the friendship of Washington, whom he had met at the time of Braddock's ill-fated expedition, he had established a medical practice and an apothecary shop at Fredericksburg. He had entered the war as colonel of the 3rd Virginia regiment, had commanded the sector of the front that faced Staten Island in the summer of 1776, and had been with Washington since the retreat from Long Island.

Arthur St. Clair, another Scot, an Edinburgh man, had fought under Amherst at Ticonderoga as an ensign. He had served in Canada in the present war and became colonel of the 2nd Pennsylvania battalion of the Continental line in January, 1776. Adam Stephen, a Virginian, had made an excellent record as lieutenant colonel of Washington's own regiment in the French and Indian War. William Alexander, who called himself Lord Stirling on the strength of his pretensions to a lapsed Scottish earldom, was born in New York. A well-to-do citizen of New Jersey, brother-in-law of that state's patriot governor, Livingston, he had entered the Continental army as a colonel in the New Jersey line. He, too, had seen service in the previous war and, like Sullivan, had been made a prisoner at Long Island.

The fifth brigade commander was Matthias Alexis de Roche de Fermoy, who had for many years enjoyed an excellent reputation as an officer of engineers in the French army and wore the cross of the Order of St. Louis. He turned out, however, to be one of several foreign military adventurers to whom the Continental Congress, with a somewhat too great confidence in imported talent, gave rank disproportionate to their abilities. The next week was to demonstrate his incapacity. Strong drink appears to have been his undoing, as it was soon to be that of Adam Stephen. It was a hard drinking, hard living age for gentlemen and those who cultivated gentlemanly habits. Doctor Rush observed of the efficient Lord Stirling that "misfortunes before the war had led him to seek relief in toddy, with which he sometimes impaired his judgment."

Several of the regimental commanders were notable

for experience and ability. John Stark, born in New Hampshire in 1728, had, like Putnam, served with distinction in Rogers's Rangers and fought as a volunteer at Bunker Hill. John Glover, master of amphibious operations, who was heading a brigade this night, had been in the war at the head of the 14th, or "Marine" regiment since the days of the siege of Boston, when they raided the islands in the harbor for cattle and supplies that were vital to the beleaguered enemy. John Haslet had led his Delaware men through all the vicissitudes of the campaign from Long Island to Pennsylvania with conspicuous gallantry. The lieutenant colonel of the 3rd Virginia regiment was Thomas Marshall, father of the future Chief Justice of the United States, who was also a member of that regiment. Colonel Paul Dudley Sargent of Massachusetts had been wounded at Bunker Hill and, since White Plains, had been in command of a brigade. Colonel Edward Hand led the Pennsylvania riflemen, a collection of those deadly sharpshooters who had become a terror to the British. It was their marksmanship that had caused the officers of the volunteer Guards battalions to substitute light muskets, called fusees or fusils, for their spontoons, a kind of half-pike, and to alter the lacings on their uniforms to correspond with those of the rank and file so that they should not be picked off at long range.

In the lower commissioned grades were Captain William Hull of unhappy memory, who was fated to surrender Detroit to the British in 1812, and Captain William Washington of the 3rd Virginia, who was soon to become an able leader of cavalry. A lieutenant in his company was eighteen-year-old James Monroe, who was about to give the invader what an orator of a later day was to describe as "the glaived hand of bloody welcome." He had been doing it ever since Harlem Heights.

One of the battery commanders was young Alexander Hamilton, who was described as "small, slender, and with a delicate frame." Though he would not be twenty until the 11th of the next month, he had already written pamphlets so forceful that they were attributed to John Jay. He had won his captaincy by examination and had fought at Long Island and in every battle since. They were his guns that covered the retirement from New Brunswick. If he followed his usual habit this night, he set his horse to helping the artillery teams and, lost in thought, with his cocked hat pulled down over his eyes, marched beside one of his cannon, absent-mindedly patting it from time to time, as if it were a favorite horse or plaything.

Washington himself, it was observed, had seemed "never so determined as now." Although the direction of the wind was such that the troops did not have to face the storm and the men did their best to protect the pans of their muskets with their blankets, many failed to keep them dry, and Sullivan sent an aide to the Commander-in-Chief to tell him that wet priming was rendering the firearms useless. "Tell General Sullivan," was Washington's reply, "to use the bayonet. I am resolved to take Trenton." And as he rode along the column, he called to the men from time to time: "Press on; press on, boys!"

· F O U R ·

O N resuming the march at Birmingham the two wings of the army separated. Sullivan led his command down the River road, which trended toward the Delaware and followed the river bank to Trenton, while Greene advanced by way of the Scotch road and then along the road from Pennington, which ran across the hills a mile or so inland. It was a little longer than the other route, a thing that Sullivan was careful to make allowance for by halting his column for a few minutes.

Four guns were placed at the head of the infantry in each column. With each advance party marched a detachment of artillery with spikes and drag ropes to disable or haul away the enemy cannon. Captain Washington's company had taken care that nobody from the Birmingham neighborhood should get ahead of the columns and carry to Trenton the news of the approaching attack. But there came a moment when it seemed as if all hope of a surprise was ruined.

In a narrow lane Greene's advance party encountered a detachment that approached from the direction of Trenton as if it were the advance guard of an enemy force. Fortunately there were no trigger-happy soldiers in Greene's leading element, for the group turned out to be the scouting party, commanded by Captain Richard Clough Anderson, father of the Anderson of Fort Sumter, that had caused the alarm in Trenton the night before and allayed Rall's fears of a more serious attack. General Stephen had sent it out on the 24th without the Commander-in-Chief's knowledge, and Washington now turned upon him furiously, exclaiming: "You, sir, may have ruined all my plans by having put them on their guard." Then, with a consideration for an unlucky officer of relatively humble rank that must be almost unique in military history, he spoke calmly and kindly to Captain Anderson and told him to march his men at the head of the column, where they would be less fatigued after the exertions they had already made than they would be in the rear.

Dawn came when the American troops were still about two miles from their destination. It was near eight o'clock and broad day when they came in sight of the Hessian outpost on the Pennington road. But sentinels are seldom on the alert in such weather, and Lieutenant Wiederhold, the commander of the advance post, just happened to step out of doors and see the line of Greene's skirmishers emerging from the woods about two hundred yards in front of him. His men fell back on their outpost; it was reinforced from the outpost on the road to Princeton. There was some brisk firing. But both outposts were compelled to retire swiftly into the town, and almost simultaneously Sullivan's advance drove in the fifty jägers stationed at General Philemon Dickenson's house on the River road.

The usual patrols had been omitted that morning, but the detachment of British Light Dragoons, between whom and their German allies no love appears to have been lost, got their horses saddled in time to ride hell-for-leather for Princeton and safety. A few minutes later and their retreat would have been cut off. For although, as Washington observed, the Hessian outposts kept up "a good retiring fire," they could not check the rush of Stephen's and de Fermoy's brigades, which swept past the entrance to the town and formed a line that completely closed the gap between the Princeton road and Assanpink Creek. The guns went into action at the junction of King and Queen Streets, the very spot where the redoubt would have been if Rall had obeyed Donop's orders. Stirling's brigade took position to support the guns, and Mercer, swinging his column off the road to the right, made contact with the left of Sullivan's line and attacked through the western outskirts of the village.

In Trenton the wretched Rall had to be called twice by his brigade adjutant before he appeared, in his nightshirt, at his bedroom window. The Lossberg regiment was already mustering behind the naked poplar trees in Church Alley; Dechow had formed his Knyphausen battalion facing Sullivan's advance in the southern quarter of the town; Rall's own regiment was falling in near the lower end of King Street. But nobody knew exactly what to do, and Knox's round shot were bounding down the streets. Shells from Hamilton's battery, which had been well back in Greene's column and was thus the last to come into position, caught the van of the Lossbergs as they emerged from Church Alley with orders to clear Queen Street, and so discouraged them that they fell back and formed in line facing northeast on the eastern edge of the village. Rall's regiment, with its colonel and colors at its head and its two guns in front of it, advanced to the attack. But the American artillery checked it halfway up King Street; Mercer's men, filtering through the tanyard and between the houses on the west side of the street, assailed its left; and it retreated in such disorder that it threw the left wing of the Lossbergs into confusion. Captain Washington's company charged the Rall regiment's guns and captured them, though he himself was wounded in both hands and Lieutenant Monroe was hit by a bullet that cut an artery in his shoulder. Knox's cannon silenced the Knyphausens' guns, which had gone into action with the Lossbergs, and the Lossbergs' pieces were so mishandled that they proved a fatal burden to the Knyphausen regiment.

Stirling's infantry raced down both King and Queen Streets, Mercer's drove through from the west. The village grew thick with a fog of blowing snow and sleet and cannon smoke. Hessian officers seeking for Rall to give them orders, groups of frantic fugitives, and squads of fierce pursuers darted through streets and lanes and among the leafless shrubbery of the gardens between and around the houses. Doors were burst in by Americans seeking for snipers in upper windows. Camp women and hangers-on and, according to angry British officers, a good many soldiers added to the confusion by trying to save plunder-laden wagons. The air was full of yells and cheers, the screams and groans of the wounded, the bang of musket shots, and the more frequent "squibbing" of flashes in the pan. For the storm soon rendered the muskets of the Hessians as useless as those of their assailants, and the fight, but for the artillery, became one of bayonets, clubbed gun butts, the halberds of the sergeants, and the spontoons and swords of the officers: "a most horrid scene to the inhabitants," as Henry Knox wrote to his wife a few days later.

Rall sent Dechow permission to fall back, if necessary, to an orchard near the position to which the Lossberg regiment had retired, and Sullivan's men made sure that he did so. With Stark's regiment leading them, the brigades of St. Clair, Sargent, and Glover drove the Knyphausens out along Second Street (now State). Glover's brigade cut the enemy's last line of retreat by seizing the bridge across the Assanpink—over which some hundreds of fugitives had already fled—and occupying the heights on the farther side.

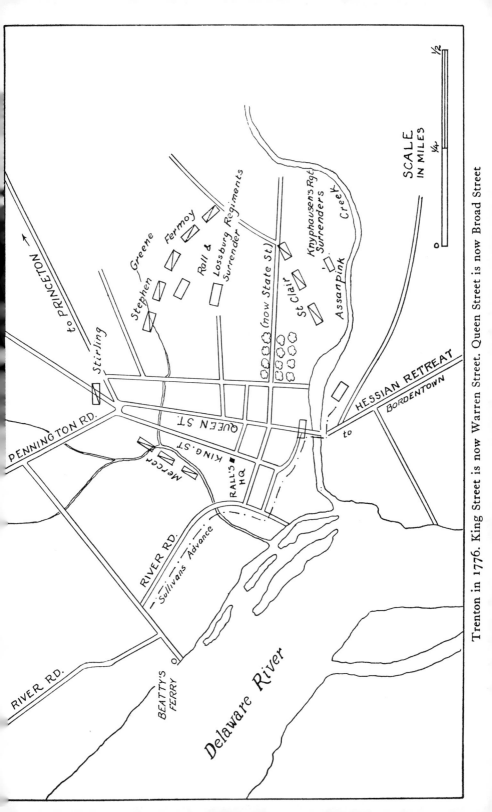

Trenton in 1776. King Street is now Warren Street. Queen Street is now Broad Street

The village was now almost entirely in American hands, but Rall, who ought to have devoted himself to saving what was left of his command, determined to retake it. He succeeded in re-forming the remains of his own regiment on the left of the Lossbergs and, with the colors in the center and the band playing them into action, led them to the attack. But Knox had brought up his guns. Forrest's battery opened on them with shell and round shot, and American riflemen ensconced in the cellars and upper windows of the houses, with pans and priming dry, stopped them with a deadly fire. The Rall regiment broke again, and Rall gave the order to the Lossbergs, who still had about two hundred men in line, to fall back to the neighborhood of the orchard.

A few minutes later he fell from his horse with two dreadful wounds in his side. The remaining field officers considered an attempt to break through to the road to Princeton or the upper fords of the Assanpink. But the solid untouched brigades of Stephen and Fermoy not only blocked the way but now, supported by the six guns of Forrest's battery, advanced in an attack that threatened annihilation. At sixty paces from the Hessian line they halted. There was a brief parley. Then down came the Hessian colors, the officers lifted their hats on their sword points in token of surrender, and the soldiers grounded their arms or, in chagrin, smashed them and flung them among the orchard trees.

Five hundred yards to the south, St. Clair's brigade, with Stark still in the van, had herded the Knyphausen regiment onto the low swampy margin of the creek, nearly half a mile to the eastward of the bridge. Dechow, mortally wounded in the left hip, had given himself up and surrendered his sword to Sullivan. The Lossberg guns, which had fatally delayed his retreat, were bogged down in the soft ground and immovable, and a crowd of bandsmen, male and female camp-followers, and wagons heaped with plunder impeded and confused the column. High ground commanded its left. On its right the creek ran bank-full and swift. It was under the fire of the guns with Glover near the farther end of the bridge; Sullivan's infantry were closing in on its rear; and in front were the troops of Greene's division.

Some of the bolder spirits in the regiment, both officers and men, broke through the thick undergrowth that bordered the stream, resolved to brave the rushing icy water rather than surrender. They were soon neck-deep. Some of them won through. A few, swept off their feet, were drowned. Others turned back. And now St. Clair's brigade came up. It halted at about forty paces and, with the humanity of the time, which forms so strange a contrast with the usages of modern war, fired a volley over the heads of the trapped regiment. Then an American officer rode forward and demanded its surrender. There was a little haggling over terms. The officers were promised the possession of their swords and baggage. The beaten soldiers threw down their muskets at the word of command. The Americans tossed their hats in the air, and their cheering answered the cheering of their comrades at the orchard, at the bridge, and in the streets of the village. It was half past nine, only about one hour and three-quarters since the first shots had been fired.

· F I V E ·

WASHINGTON was riding down King Street, and near by the mortally wounded Rall was being carried into his quarters, when Major Wilkinson galloped up with the news that the Knyphausen regiment had surrendered.

"This is a glorious day for our country, Major Wilkinson!" Washington exclaimed happily and shook the young officer by the hand. There have, indeed, been few days more glorious. "It may be doubted," writes Trevelyan in *The American Revolution*, "whether so small a number of men ever employed so short a space of time with greater and more lasting results upon the history of the world." Yet the cost in killed and wounded had been astonishingly light: a hundred and six of the Hessians; and of the Americans, none killed, and only Captain Washington and Lieutenant Monroe and two enlisted men wounded.

Washington and Greene visited the dying Rall, gave him such consolation as they could, and took his parole. In his pocket was found the note of warning he had thrust away the night before. On hearing its contents the unhappy man exclaimed: "If I had read this at Mr. Hunt's, I would not be here now!" Through an interpreter he begged Washington to treat his men kindly, and Washington assured him that he would do so. Rall died next day, and the zealous Dechow, who might have wished to live in order to defend himself from blame that was not his, survived him by only a few hours.

Meanwhile the prisoners were assembled, skulking fugitives routed out of attics, barns, and outbuildings, and the wounded among them paroled, since the Americans had no means of transportation for them. The captured wagons and the forty sound horses were needed to haul the thousand fine muskets, the twelve brass-barrel drums, the full set of band instruments, and the six excellent field guns that had also been taken.

It was ordered that the portmanteaus of the Hessian officers and the knapsacks of the men should be restored to them without being searched or even opened. Their loot was collected, and word was sent around for all who had been plundered to come in and claim their possessions. Forty hogsheads of rum, which were among the spoil, Washington ordered to be staved in and poured on the ground, but not before a good many of his men had carried an impromptu celebration of the victory to a point where their efficiency for further military action seemed doubtful.

Their condition, indeed, was such that at a council of war which was held later that morning several officers put it forward as one of several reasons against attempting to take immediate advantage of the present success. Knox and Greene urged that the fleeing enemy be pursued at once and cited instances from military history to support their opinion. But others pointed out that it would be unwise to risk spoiling the effect of the victory by a subsequent reverse; that there was a strong British battalion at Princeton, which would be on the flank of any movement down the river; and that Donop's troops, of whose wide dispersal news had not yet reached American headquarters, outnumbered the force that Washington could bring against them. A considerable detachment of troops, moreover, would be required to guard the prisoners, whose number was equal to more than a third of the men Washington had with him, and it could not be denied that both the prisoners and the booty would be much safer on the other side of the river.

Regretfully Washington gave the order to retire, and soon after midday the long column of prisoners took the road to McKonkey's ferry under guard of Stirling's brigade. The fight and the victory had slaked the Americans' thirst for vengeance. Stirling, who had been made a prisoner by these very regiments, treated them, he wrote to Governor Livingston, "in such style as will make the rest of them more willing to surrender than fight." Compared with their ill-nourished, threadbare and shoeless captors, they looked hearty and well-clad. But they had been told that the Americans killed and ate their prisoners, and fear mingled with the shame they felt at their defeat.

The rest of the army followed them. The storm, still unabated, now blew in the faces of the soldiers. The road was the worse for the trampling Sullivan's column had given it early that morning. The river was still high and raging, the ice more dangerous than it had been. It was near dark before the first troops were ferried over, deep night and bitterly cold when the last were crossing. A boatload of Hessian officers came close to being swamped; three American soldiers were said to have been frozen to death. By the time the troops were back in their old quarters all of them had been marching and fighting for thirty-six hours, some for forty hours, and some for fifty, and there were organizations that had covered forty miles. It is not surprising that a thousand of them, more than two-fifths of the whole command, were reported unfit for duty next morning.

Their commander did not grudge them their rest. They had done all and borne all that he had asked them to do and bear, and they would cheerfully have gone on doing and enduring, if he had called on them to do so. But what had weighed with Washington most heavily in deciding to retire had been the fatigue of the exertions they had already made. In General Orders this morning he congratulated them on their behavior and "with pleasure observed that he had been in many actions, but always perceived some misbehavior in some individuals, but in that action he saw none." It was not their fault that the offensive had not accomplished all that had been hoped of it.

For it had to be admitted, of course, that it had been incomplete. If Cadwalader had been able to get his troops over from Bristol as ordered, Washington could have moved against Donop with confidence that he could give battle with at least equal numbers. But the flooding tide had packed the ice against the New Jersey shore in a three-hundred-foot-wide mass which was impenetrable to Cadwalader's boats and over which it was impossible to move his artillery. Ewing's failure to cross at the Trenton ferry, however, seems actually to have contributed to the victory. It is true that if Ewing had succeeded in crossing unseen and had been able to keep his men concealed on the shore until Washington made his attack, he could have seized the bridge over the Assanpink and so made prisoners of those who escaped. But concealment would have been extremely difficult after daylight came—the Hessians had an outpost at the bridge and another beyond it on the road to the ferry, with guards on the river bank—and discovery before Washington's troops attacked would have meant not only the destruction of Ewing's little force but that the whole Hessian command would have been under arms and on the alert when Washington reached the outposts west of the village.

As the hours went by, moreover, and reports came in from down the river, it became clear that the results of the offensive were better than had been understood. Cadwalader, who, in ignorance of Washington's retirement, had succeeded in landing his troops on the Jersey shore on the afternoon of the 26th, sent word that Donop was in full retreat. Soon after, came the news that something like consternation reigned among the British at Princeton and New Brunswick. Washington packed his prisoners off to Philadelphia—the soldiers on foot, the officers in post-chaises—to be paraded through the streets, with their captured arms and colors behind them lest any stubborn Tory should doubt the reports of his success, then turned his attention to a movement that should gather and increase the harvest it had won for him.

CHAPTER III

Lord Cornwallis Fails to "Bag the Fox"

· O N E ·

BACK in September—about the time, curiously enough, when Henry Knox was promising his wife that one defeat would mean ruin to the British—Sir Henry Clinton wrote in what he called an observation: "My advice has ever been to avoid even the possibility of a check. We live by victory. Are we sure of it this day? *J'en doute* [*sic*]." Clinton had taken what was tantamount to a beating at Charleston and was correspondingly anxious, though he believed that Washington's defeat on Long Island had destroyed the rebels' confidence in their chief. One British victory had followed another, until in mid-December Donop's division stood on the eastern bank of the Delaware and Sir Henry was so snugly quartered in Rhode Island that he had time to concern himself with getting a supply of suitable table linen from New York.

The capture of Newport was exploited in dispatches as the crowning success of a brilliant campaign. General Howe sent an aide-de-camp to the King with the glorious news. In England it was already believed that the war was about over. Horace Walpole, who had no love for the existing government, wrote his friend Horace Mann that only the armed intervention of France could save the Americans from submission, and Edmund Burke expected Consols to leap upward as soon as the close friends of the Cabinet had made arrangements to profit by the official announcement that the rebellion had been crushed.

As Howe viewed the situation at the end of November, Clinton would advance on Boston next summer with 10,000 men, while 2000 occupied Providence; a force of 10,000 would advance up the Hudson, leaving a garrison of 5000 to occupy New York; 8000 would hold New Jersey until an autumn campaign took Philadelphia; and South Carolina and Georgia would be conquered the following winter.

All this, to be sure, would require at least ten ships-of-the-line, another battalion of artillery, more company officers, three hundred more horses and saddles —Irish horses preferred, since they were hardier and better at fences—and 15,000 troops from Russia or Hanover and the other German states. Three weeks later, cutting his garment more nearly according to his cloth, Howe wrote Lord George Germain that his main offensive in the spring would be against Pennsylvania, with 10,000 men, and he appears to have expected to be able to complete that campaign in time to cooperate with Burgoyne's advance from Canada, which would not be able to reach Albany before mid-September.

In the meanwhile he saw nothing to prevent his indulgence in what Major Wilkinson described euphemistically as "the pleasures of the long room and the faro table." His optimism permeated the army. Sir Henry Clinton planned to go home for a few months in *H.M.S. Asia* in January. Lord Cornwallis packed his portmanteaus and sent them aboard ship for a visit to his ailing wife. The wives of some of the other officers braved the miseries of the winter passage of the Atlantic to join their husbands in New York. And the troops in general settled down for the cold weather with that talent for making themselves comfortable in a foreign land which has ever been a characteristic of a British army abroad.

It cannot have been easy to do this in New York in the winter of 1776-77. The British had hardly occupied the city, when, on the night of September 20th, it burst into flames. Starting in the neighborhood of Whitehall, the fire spread swiftly, although boatloads of sailors from the warships helped the troops in their fight against it. For the weather had been dry, most of the roofs were made of cedar shingles, and a strong south wind was blowing. One patriot, moreover, saw it break out in several places, and there were incendiaries, caught in the act, whom the infuriated British soldiers bayoneted, hung up by the heels, or threw, living, into the flames. A good many persons were arrested and charged with setting the fire, but they were released after brief examination. For there was no evidence that the conflagration had been due to orders issued by Washington, as at first had been believed.

Nearly five hundred buildings were destroyed. The hundred-and-eighty-foot spire of Trinity Church blazed like a gigantic exclamation point until it crashed in crackling embers. Almost the whole district from the Battery to St. Paul's between Broadway and the Hudson, and between Broadway and the East River as far as Broad Street, became and remained throughout the British occupation a mass of black unsightly rubble. When the ruins cooled, a labyrinth of shanties built of old boards, poles, and discarded sailcloth turned the area of vacant walls and tottering chimneys into a slum that was infested by drunkards, prostitutes, runaway Negroes, and the sweepings of the waterfront. "Canvass Town" was the name it went by, and one who had seen it as a boy remembered it as "the Wapping, St. Giles, and the Five Points of the desolated garrisoned city."

Chimney fires became so frequent that the British military governor was moved to appoint six chimney inspectors. He ordered severe penalties for soldiers convicted of pulling down houses and fences and injuring the property of any inhabitant. A private was sentenced to death for plundering. But known sympathizers with the patriot cause had a broad letter R, for rebel, chalked on their doors and went in fear of the retribution that their Tory neighbors promised them. The churches of the Dissenters were turned into prisons and hospitals. One of them became a riding school.

To escape from the dreariness of their surroundings the troops, officers and men alike, turned to gambling, drinking, and whoring. Howe permitted the presence of six camp women with each company, and local talent was not lacking. The army chaplains of the time were seldom present with their organizations, and there was no regular medical service, only a surgeon and a surgeon's mate attached to each regiment. Food was cheap and good: beef could be bought for three pence ha' penny the pound. But fuel was scarce, and early in December *The New York Gazette and Daily Mercury*, which was published by Hugh Gaine at The Bible and Crown, printed a report that the coal ships from Louisburg had been captured by rebel privateers.

Armed vessels, sailing under letters of marque from the Continental Congress or individual states, were a continual embarrassment and threat to the King's forces in America. Clinton, in his expedition against

Charleston, had been without orders for four months because dispatches from Howe had been thrown overboard from the *Glasgow* man-of-war in an action with a rebel fleet. A row galley took one of his transports, and he was desperately anxious about the rest of them on the way back to New York. Massachusetts had the sloop *Freedom* cruising from Newfoundland as far south as latitude 38° in search of prizes. Another American privateer attacked a British transport at sea and took it, although the seven hundred and fifty Highlanders whom it carried put up a gallant fight. Several captured American vessels were brought into New York in October; *H.M.S. Galatea* was reported near the end of November to have taken fifteen or sixteen prizes; but Clinton heard that many large privateers were still at large.

Life on the British transports was such as to make the passengers glad to reach any port, and it grew worse as the winter storms prolonged the voyage. The ships were shorthanded, for the service was unpopular, the Navy's press gangs did not scruple to kidnap men from the transports, and the sailors seized every opportunity to desert their vessels in America. At Cork the loaders of supply ships struck. Ships themselves were hard to find, since they were likely to be detained in American ports and could get no cargoes to carry home.

An officer of the Guards, describing his voyage, wrote of "continued destruction in the fore-tops, the pox above-board, the plague between decks, hell in the forecastle, and the devil at the helm." Scurvy was endemic. Some men died, and the number of deaths in the cargoes of horses was almost ruinous. Excepting the recruits from Scotland, where the war was popular, the new drafts, with their large infusion of jail birds and criminals of every sort, behaved abominably, refused to embark, deserted whenever possible, and fought fierce battles among themselves. Arrived at New York, such men, naturally, did nothing to improve the discipline and morals of the garrison.

Nor was the example of the Commander-in-Chief of His Majesty's forces in America such as to accomplish that purpose. Two centuries earlier, Francis Bacon had written: "I know not how, but martiall men are given to love: I think it is but as they are given to wine, for perils commonly aske to be paid in pleasures"; and Sir William Howe was no exception. On his return to the city on December 16th he gave himself up to a ten days' celebration of his successes, to preparations for the reception of the red ribbon of the Order of the Bath, with which he had been rewarded by his grateful sovereign, and to the delights of his mistress, Mrs. Josiah Loring, who was described as a "flashing blond."

She was the wife of the former high sheriff of Dorchester, Massachusetts. When the British evacuated Boston, she had accompanied Howe to Halifax and thence to New York, and she remained with him throughout his stay in America. Her husband held the position of Commissary of Prisoners and made a very good thing out of it, as the pale faces at the barred windows of the sugar house on Crown Street (now Liberty) and the rotting captives in the prison hulks in the harbor bore witness. She queened it in the ballroom of the City Tavern and, sharing her lover's fondness for high play, took delight in hundred-guinea stakes.

Angry loyalists, like Judge Thomas Jones, who believed that Howe had lost his one golden opportunity

of winning the war by his failure to advance on Philadelphia, might sneer at the General's amorous diver-
sions, his gunning, and his feasting. A contemporary
versifier might exhort:

> "Awake, awake, Sir Billy,
>   There's forage on the plain.
>   Ah, leave your little filly,
>   And open the campaign."

Across the sea, Robert Burns might comment:

> "Poor Tammy Gage within a cage
>   Was kept at Boston ha', man;
>   Till Willy Howe took o'er the knowe
>   For Philiadelphiá, man;
>   Wi' sword and gun he thought a sin
>   Guid Christian bluid to draw, man;
>   But at New York wi' knife and fork
>   Sir-Loin he hackéd sma', man."

But Howe was sublimely confident of the future, per-
fectly content with the present. With his mistress at
his side he could read in *The New York Gazette and
Daily Mercury* that his wife had been "most graciously
received" by Their Majesties at St. James's and could
feel that he had made the best of both worlds.

More innocent amusements, also, were not lacking
both for him and his officers. Tory society in the city
was gay. As long as the evenings were mild enough the
army bands played in Trinity Churchyard, while the
officers, the local belles, and their beaux promenaded
in front of the ruins of the church. There each day took
place the colorful ceremony of guard mounting. The
Highlanders would march on in low checkered bonnets,

red coats, tartans, and kilts, with broadswords and dirks in addition to their bayoneted muskets. Or it might be the Hessians with their grotesque exaggerations of military pomp, or perhaps a detail of a British line regiment, their red coats crossed by broad white belts, with facings of yellow or blue, and their officers in long scarlet sashes and gorgets that were often of gold and engraved with the regimental crest. And there was the studio on William Street, where John Ramage, the painter of minatures, took charming likenesses of young ladies and their cavaliers.

Gaine's *Gazette* advertised a pamphlet entitled *The True-Interest of America impartially Stated*, which was said to contain "certain strictures on a pamphlet entitled *Common Sense*." Somebody wrote and published a play, *The Battle of Brooklyn, A Farce in Two Acts*, which caused much laughter among those who were regarded as right-thinking people. Best of all, preparations were being made to reopen the theater on John Street, which had been closed since the outbreak of hostilities because the Continental Congress considered such amusements too frivolous for the times. It was renamed The Theatre Royal. Doctor Beaumont, the Surgeon General, became manager and principal low comedian. Officers with "talent and inclination" were requested to send in their names for parts. Female rôles were generally played by young lieutenants or ensigns, but certain of the women who had "followed the drum" were sometimes paid two, three, or four guineas for each performance.

That well-tried old favorite, Henry Fielding's *Tom Thumb*, was chosen as the opening piece. Captain Oliver Delancy of the 17th Light Dragoons went to work at painting the scenery; Captain Stanley wrote a special prologue. Tickets could be bought at The Bible and Crown. The playbills bore the heading "Charity" or "For the benefit of orphans and widows of soldiers," and it was understood that the orphans and widows of soldiers killed in this war were meant.

Such was life for the British in New York when, on December 28th, disquieting rumors of untoward events on the Delaware ran through the town. Two days later the *New York Gazette* made the following laconic announcement of what almost everybody already knew:

"Wednesday morning last one of the Hessian brigades stationed at Trenton was surprised by a large body of rebels, and after an engagement that lasted a little time, three or four hundred made good their retreat, and the whole loss was about nine hundred men."

By the next day it was all over town that Washington, who had lately been reported as in flight to Lancaster, while his men were throwing down their arms, had entered New Jersey with sixty thousand troops.

· T W O ·

IN the dawn of Friday, December 27th, the day after the battle of Trenton, three weary officers and fifty exhausted men stumbled into Leslie's lines at Princeton to confirm the news of the disaster, of which some hint had been brought by the fleeing dragoons on the previous day. They were members of the Knyphausen regiment who had made good their escape across the Assanpink at the end of the fighting and had missed the way to Bordentown in the stormy night.

With them came the first wisps of the fog of war. In the next four days it rolled swiftly and ever more densely along the British front, enveloping one after another of those "rather large links" in Howe's line of communications until it wrapped his headquarters in New York in a shroud of uncertainty and apprehension.

Before Friday night Grant at New Brunswick had the bad news and also word that Donop was in full retreat. Not yet altogether aware of the significance of the event, Grant wrote to Donop about "the most unfortunate affair" at Trenton in a letter that crackled with suppressed anger and thinly veiled contempt. He had not thought, he said, that all the rebels in America could have taken that brigade prisoners, and as to Donop's retirement: ". . . if I was [*sic*] with you, your Grenadiers and Yagers, I should not be afraid of an attack from Washington's army, which is almost naked and does not exceed 8000 men." He had sent an express to General Howe, and until he received orders for future arrangements, he concluded, "I must beg you to remain at Allentown [whither Donop had retired] or if that should not be practicable, for I don't know the place, you must crowd into Princeton, Maidenhead, Cranbury, and Kingston."

About the same time, the unhappy Donop was writing to explain his movement to Lieutenant General von Knyphausen, his superior officer in the Hessian contingent. The mob of panic-stricken fugitives which had poured into Bordentown the previous morning had told of the presence of "many thousands" of rebels at Trenton, and patrols sent in that direction had seemed to confirm that report. Donop's ammunition had run low: only about nine cartridges to a cannon, and very few for the muskets. He understood that a strong rebel force was advancing on Princeton, he heard nothing from

General Leslie, and he saw himself in danger of being cut off. But he did not state what was probably the most cogent reason for his retirement to Allentown: namely, that he had dispersed his forces so widely that he could not concentrate them nearer the enemy in time to meet the emergency as he understood it.

He reported that he had brought off all his baggage, but, though he had commandeered every wagon he could find, had been compelled to abandon a large quantity of rations. He did not mention the fact that he had left his sick and wounded behind him. He had, indeed, stood not upon the order of his going. But his troops, characteristically enough, had found time to destroy the library of Francis Hopkinson, a signer of the Declaration of Independence, and to pillage other houses in Bordentown before their hasty departure on the morning of the 27th.

Before the dawn of the following day, however, the British attitude toward Donop's retreat had undergone a complete change. At Princeton rumors and reports of the enemy's movements must have given General Leslie a bad night. For at two o'clock in the morning of the 28th he sent a messenger galloping to Allentown with an order for Donop to join him "without loss of time." A force of fourteen hundred rebels, he heard, had landed at Trenton and were marching by way of Pennington to Rocky Hill with the intention of joining certain New Jersey troops there in an attack on Princeton, and three hours later Leslie repeated his order to Donop by a second messenger.

At New Brunswick Grant also was alarmed by this time. The retreat and pursuit of Washington across New Jersey makes it misleadingly easy to regard the

British front as consisting of no more than the Trenton-Burlington area. But actually, of course, it extended all the way from the Hudson to the Delaware, and the fact that the British line of communications and supply ran parallel to it made their position highly vulnerable. An enemy force at Rocky Hill could cut the main road between Princeton and New Brunswick at Kingston by a march of only a couple of miles.

Grant echoed Leslie's order to Donop, called a Hessian battalion to Princeton from Amboy, and grew anxious for the safety of those heavy guns for whose arrival Donop had been waiting in order to deal with Seymour's flotilla at Burlington. There followed two or three days of feverish marching and countermarching, of fruitless scouting, and of standing to arms in the bitterly cold hours before dawn, as each rumor of the American movements contradicted the one before it. Leslie was ordered to occupy Kingston and to send the redoubtable 42nd Foot to Rocky Hill, with outposts in the direction of Pluckemin, while the light infantry moved out on the Trenton road to screen Donop's march from Allentown. But the next day Kingston was occupied by two of Donop's battalions, the 42nd was posted a little to the south of Princeton to cover the line of Stony Brook, and the light infantry moved on to Maidenhead.

Donop had obeyed his orders promptly, sending his baggage to Cranbury under guard of a hundred grenadiers and arriving at Princeton with the rest of his command at two o'clock on the afternoon of the 28th. Since the village was already overcrowded, four hundred of his men had to sleep in the open that night. "You can imagine what must happen to my men," he complained to Grant. "All sick." His baggage train came in on the 29th but was not permitted to be unpacked, and nobody was made any happier by learning that a belated detachment of his command had been attacked and had suffered the loss of a company guidon, several men taken prisoners, and an officer killed. Next day, not far from the village, a British baggage train, a commissary, and a patrol of dragoons were captured by an enemy scouting party. The rebels seemed to be roving the country at will. On the 29th, moreover, came rumors that Washington was advancing with his whole army. Donop ordered two small redoubts to be constructed to cover the approach from Stony Brook to the village, and the troops at Kingston were instructed to march in and occupy the high ground around Nassau Hall at the slightest alarm.

· T H R E E ·

ALL that had actually happened on the American side thus far was that Cadwalader had succeeded in crossing the Delaware about a mile above Bristol on the 27th and had taken advantage of Donop's withdrawal, and on the 29th Washington had begun his second crossing. Cadwalader's movement required considerable moral courage on his part. For only after he was over the river did he get a full account of the Hessian retreat, and that news was balanced by the puzzling intelligence that after the victory at Trenton Washington had returned to Pennsylvania.

Should Cadwalader go on? Or, since he was in ignorance of Washington's intentions, ought he not to draw back across the river and wait for orders? Several of his officers urged the latter course. But his men were spoiling for a fight, of which they had already been once disappointed; the New England troops had been cheered by an issue of shoes, stockings, and breeches, of which they had been in dire need; and the ardent spirit of their commander, Colonel Daniel Hitchcock, was such that he rode at their head, though he was in the last stages of consumption and lived only two weeks longer. Moreover, Colonel Reed, who had spent the previous night in concealment in a house in Bordentown, receiving the reports of spies on Donop's movements, was all for advancing.

Cadwalader was an able officer and a patriot who never failed to place the good of the cause before his personal advancement. Twice he refused a general's commission in the Continental army. He had been in the fighting on the Hudson, had been taken prisoner and exchanged. He was endowed with good courage and a high heart, but with prudence as well. So he had compromised and was retiring down the river to Burlington to await developments, when, in the late afternoon, he received orders from Washington to defer offensive action pending further instructions.

From Burlington at ten that night he wrote the Commander-in-Chief, with hardly suppressed jubilation, to report that the "great precipitation" of the enemy's departure had moved him "to proceed, though not quite conformable to your orders which I received on the march this afternoon." A pursuit would keep up their panic, he went on and, suggesting that Washington might think proper to join him, he added: "If we can drive them from West Jersey, the success will raise an army next spring and establish the credit of the Continental money to support it."

Not an enemy soldier had been encountered in the circuitous and cautious march to Burlington. Excepting the sick and wounded men whom Donop had left in a small and very dirty hospital, none were to be found at Bordentown, when Cadwalader advanced to that place next day. The people there said that the Hessians had retreated to Hide Town, which was probably some Hessian soldier's rendering of Hightstown, and the energetic Reed, who pushed on to Trenton before daylight that morning with only two or three companions, saw not a single enemy, though the inhabitants were, naturally, anxious and fearful after their first-hand experience of war earlier in the week.

On the following day, Sunday, December 29th, Mifflin came over with sixteen hundred more of the Pennsylvania militia and Captain Procter's battery and established his headquarters at Bordentown. Cadwalader, whose force now comprised twenty-one hundred men, two brass six-pounders, and two three-pounders of iron, moved out to Crosswicks, thence to keep up the good work of harassing and confusing the enemy by means of strong and daring scouting parties, which he had begun soon after landing on the Jersey shore.

It was one of these that so discomfited Donop's detachment on its march to Princeton. Another party arrived at Cranbury with the intention of pushing on to New Brunswick on horseback and liberating General Lee, who was in confinement there. They had understood that the place was now held by only two hundred and fifty men. But scouts brought word that the garrison had been reinforced by fifteen hundred, and they fell back to Allentown for the first day's rest Cadwalader had given his men since they crossed the river. He instructed his command, however, to be ready to march at a moment's notice, and at Bordentown Mifflin issued orders for the preparation of three days' cooked rations. For Washington was back in Trenton again by the 30th, and orders for a general offensive were expected from hour to hour.

From Trenton on the 29th Reed had sent Washington word of the situation he had found there. Other information had already decided Washington to return, and that same day he again began the crossing of the river. Again the drifting ice made the passage dangerous and slow. Not until the afternoon of the following day was it completed. The roads were heavy with the remains of the recent sleet and snow. And again the delay might well mean the failure of the whole enterprise. For with the passage of every hour the British must be recovering from their confusion, bringing the concentration of their troops to completion: Howe himself was reported to be advancing from Amboy with a thousand light infantry.

Worse still was the uncertainty as to the number of veteran troops who would remain with the colors after the expiration of their terms of enlistment with the end of the year, and it took another day to find that out. With his headquarters at Trenton, Washington had the little war-worn regiments paraded and addressed them one by one, telling them that their splendid victory of the week before would go for nought if it were not followed up, promising each man a bounty of ten dollars for another six weeks of service, and pledging his private fortune for its payment, since $50,000 in Continental currency, which Morris and his friends in Philadelphia had raised for the army, had not yet reached him.

"I feel the inconvenience of this advance," he wrote to the President of the Congress, "and know the consequences which will result from it; but what could be done? Pennsylvania had allowed the same to her militia; the troops felt their importance, and would have their price." And he added, with his customary fairmindedness: "Indeed, as their aid is so essential, and not to be dispensed with, it is to be wondered at, that they did not estimate it at a higher rate." "I thought it no time to stand upon trifles," he wrote to Morris the same day, "when a body of firm troops, inured to danger, was absolutely necessary to lead on the more raw and undisciplined."

Knox's great voice followed that of the Commander-in-Chief. Mifflin, "on a noble looking horse, in a coat made of rose-colored blanket, with a large fur cap on his head," rode over from Bordentown to speak with the eloquence that had roused the ardor of the Pennsylvania militiamen. The dying Hitchcock exhorted his Rhode Islanders and Massachusetts men. And the soldiers, looking, as one observer said, like a flock of "animated scarecrows," stood in their ranks and listened, with the result that about fourteen or fifteen hundred of the men with Washington and about an equal number of Hitchcock's brigade "poised their firelocks" to signify their willingness to remain.

One comforting circumstance of the affair was that, as Washington wrote to Hancock: "Congress, apprehensive of this event, had made unlimited provision for it." On the 27th, before the news of the victory at Trenton had reached Baltimore, the Congress had, in fact, conferred on Washington the powers of a military dictator. And, "Happy is it for this country," ran a passage in the letter transmitting their resolution, "that the General of their forces can safely be entrusted with the most unlimited power, and neither personal security, liberty nor property be in the least degree endangered thereby."

It was an honor and a mark of confidence that would have turned the head of a Gates, an Arnold, or a Charles Lee. To the Committee of the Congress at Philadelphia Washington wrote of it: "Instead of thinking myself freed of all civil obligations, by this mark of confidence, I shall constantly bear in mind, that as the sword was the last resort for the preservation of our liberties, so it ought to be the first thing laid aside, when those liberties are firmly established."

Upon Washington's recommendation Congress made Knox a brigadier general with entire command of the artillery, and the Commander-in-Chief thanked him for his services in public orders. "This," Knox wrote to his wife from "Delaware River, near Trenton" on December 28th, "I should blush to mention to any other than you, my dear Lucy, and I am fearful that even my Lucy may think her Harry possesses a species of little vanity for doing [it] at all."

Five days later, on January 2nd, 1777, he wrote her that the men were "in high spirits, but want rum and clothing." He said nothing of the tension of that day, but it must have been felt by every officer and man, down to the dullest rear-rank private. For with every day's intelligence of the enemy's movements it had become more clear that the delay in recrossing the river had cost them most of the material advantages gained by the victory of the previous week, and the General's orders and dispositions this morning made it plain that battle was close at hand.

Colonel Reed, with a dozen Philadelphia light horsemen—they were the party that had captured the wagon train and the patrol of light dragoons on the Quaker road—had been prevented by vigilant outposts from getting close to Princeton, but they brought in word that the enemy was about to advance against Trenton, and a spy gave Cadwalader the same information. On New Year's Day, Grant, leaving only six hundred men to guard his stores and a military chest of £70,000 at New Brunswick, joined Leslie and Donop at Princeton, and that same evening Cornwallis arrived there and assumed command of a force which, with the men he brought with him, amounted to about eight thousand. Among them were some of the finest troops in the British army. His artillery numbered twenty-eight guns and included several twelve-pounders.

Washington was now in a dilemma. Gone was all hope of destroying piecemeal the scattered elements of Donop's brigade or nibbling off another link of Howe's chain of posts by capturing Princeton before its garrison could be reinforced. To retreat across the river once more or to give battle where he stood, with an army of which more than half consisted of inexperienced and untried militia, seemed to be the only courses open to him.

"Our situation was most critical and our force small," he wrote to the President of the Congress a few days later. "To remove immediately was again destroying every dawn of hope, which had begun to revive in the breasts of the Jersey militia; and to bring those troops, who had first crossed the Delaware and were lying at Crosswicks under General Cadwalader, and those under General Mifflin at Bordentown (amounting in the whole to about three thousand, six hundred), to Trenton, was to bring them to an exposed place. One or the other, however, was unavoidable. The latter was preferred, and they were ordered to join us at Trenton, which they did, by a night march, on the 1st instant."

Cadwalader had some trouble in enforcing discipline among his now very weary Pennsylvanians. Having been called out on a false alarm on one occasion, they were negligent and dilatory in responding the next time the drums beat the long roll. He admonished them paternally in brigade orders, and through mud that was almost up to their knees they joined Mifflin's force from Bordentown in arriving at Trenton early in the morning of January 2nd.

Added to the fifteen hundred Washington already had with him, these troops brought his numbers up to about fifty-two hundred men. His guns, including the six pieces captured from the Hessians and those of Procter's Pennsylvania battery, now numbered about forty. He set his troops to fortifying the eastern bank of the Assanpink so as to guard the bridge and the fords for a distance of about three miles from the point where the creek entered the Delaware and moved his headquarters from loyalist Major Barnes's house to Jonathan Richmond's tavern on the farther side of the stream. He sent General de Fermoy, with Hand's riflemen, the German battalion, Colonel Charles Scott's Virginia Continentals, and Forrest's battery up the road toward Maidenhead under orders to delay the British advance as much as possible, and proceeded to await the outcome with that appearance of unruffled confidence of which he was a master.

· F O U R ·

CHARLES STEDMAN, the young Philadelphia tory, who was a commissary with the British at this time, gave Howe rather less than his due when, eighteen years later, he wrote of the General as showing "irresolution, if not infatuation" after the Trenton disaster and accused him of allowing "an interval of eight days" to elapse before taking action. The effects of the defeat were, to be sure, profound and reached far beyond the British headquarters. Tryon confessed in a letter to Lord George Germain that it had caused him "more chagrin than any other circumstance [of] this war." The overblown reputation of the Hessians was ruined forever. Thenceforth even bands of farmers did not hesitate to attack them unless they were supported by British troops. The British authorities instructed their agents in Germany to try to get men who could shoot. General von Heister, the ranking Hessian officer in America, wrote his sovereign, whom he addressed as "Merciful Father of the Country," deploring and endeavoring to extenuate the disaster. But the small list of casualties told a deadly tale. Germain wrote von Heister: "It is to be hoped that the dangerous practice of underestimating the enemy may make a lasting impression on the rest of the army." An angry prince called von Heister home, and the unfortunate man, whose only fault had been to urge Rall's assignment to the position at Trenton, died of mortification a few months later. Howe had written Germain on December

31st: "Rall's defeat has put us much out of our way. His misconduct is amazing."

But as for the subsequent delay, actually only five days elapsed between the arrival of the news of the defeat at New York and the completion of the British dispositions that deprived Washington of the initiative; and Cornwallis gave the true reason for the rather slow mobilization in writing to Germain: "Our quarters were too much exposed. It was necessary to assemble our troops." The assembly of his army at Princeton in so short a time, considering the wide distribution of the British forces and the condition of the roads, was not discreditable. He himself covered the fifty miles from New York on horseback between morning and night.

He pushed his outposts out as far as Eight Mile Run that evening, and the watch fires of their supports could be seen shining along the road to Maidenhead where it climbed the hill south of Stony Brook. He slept at Morven, ordered his baggage train to return to New Brunswick, and was off for Trenton before daylight of the 2nd, with his troops in three columns that marched abreast along the road and across the fields on both sides of it.

Mawhood's brigade—the 17th, 40th, and 55th infantry regiments—fifty dismounted troopers of the 17th Light Dragoons, and a couple of guns were left at Princeton to guard his rear, with orders for Mawhood to join the main force with two of the infantry regiments next day. When Cornwallis reached Maidenhead, he directed Leslie to remain at that place and gave him orders similar to Mawhood's for the morrow. These detachments left him some fifty-five hundred men, with whom and the rest of his artillery he continued the march.

But his advance was slow. A heavy rain during the night had made the highway almost as deep in mud as the fields that bordered it. The men sank halfway to their knees; the guns continually threatened to bog down; and the columns had no more than left Maidenhead behind them when the Jägers and the light infantry, who covered the advance, were held up by the dreaded fire of the long American rifles, which neither the British Brown Bess nor the short German rifle could contend against successfully at long range.

At every turn of the road, from every flanking thicket and ravine, the bullets whistled. Frequently the march had to be halted until troops of the advance guard could be deployed to clarify the situation, and when they had done so, the opposition simply melted away and had to be dealt with afresh at the next natural obstacle. At Shabakunk Creek, three miles from Trenton, the advance had to be made across open fields in the face of heavy fire from Hand's riflemen, the musketry of the other American troops with them, and the shells and solid shot of Forrest's battery on the southern bank, which was densely wooded. De Fermoy apparently lost his nerve and went back to Trenton. But Colonel Hand assumed command in his place and put up a stout defense. The British advance guard and flanking parties were driven back and even pursued. Cornwallis was compelled to deploy his columns and form line of battle. But when his troops reached the farther bank, they found the woods empty, the enemy nowhere in sight.

All this, to be sure, entailed only a few casualties. The Americans, who took some prisoners, had two or three officers wounded and a few enlisted men killed. The Hessians lost fifteen, the ghost of one of whom was a terror to the Negroes of the neighborhood for many years to come. But the fighting, added to the condition of the road, forced the British to take ten hours to traverse ten miles, and every hour lost by Cornwallis was an hour gained for Washington. It was ten in the morning when Hand began his delaying tactics, three in the afternoon when the British reached a ravine one mile from their objective. And there, behind slight entrenchments, the Virginians and Forrest's battery, reinforced by four additional guns, made another determined stand.

Washington, accompanied by Greene and Knox, rode up to encourage them to hold on till the last possible minute. Greene took charge of the defense. Again Cornwallis had to deploy his columns and unlimber his guns. Another precious hour had passed, and the musket flashes were sparkling through the early winter twilight, when the Americans fell back, firing between the houses and among the garden shrubbery at the enemy columns that drove down King and Queen Streets to cut them off from the bridge.

It was a close race at the finish, though the New England brigade crossed the creek to cover the retreat, opened its ranks to let the Virginians through, and then retired, firing as they went. But Forrest had got his guns across and, with those of Moulder's battery and others already in position, checked the pursuit. The New Englanders poured helter-skelter between the railings of the narrow bridge and, as they did so, were reassured by the sight of Washington on his white horse, which stood with its breast pressed against the end of one of the bridge's rails. His countenance, as one of them remembered it, looked "firm, composed, and majestic."

About the seriousness of the brief combat that followed there is some difference of opinion. Washington called it a cannonade. Wilkinson made no mention of it in his memoirs: but Wilkinson was with St. Clair's troops, who were a couple of miles away, guarding the upper fords. Knox wrote to his Lucy that the American artillery "saluted" the enemy at this juncture "with great vociforation and some execution." But it is clear that a British column was driven back by the New Englanders at the lower fords, and a Connecticut officer saw another column repulsed three times in its efforts to storm the bridge, though it was supported by artillery and the officers beat their men with the flat of their swords to drive them forward. He guessed their losses at about a hundred and fifty, and a historian of the present day estimates the British killed and wounded in this "second battle of Trenton" at not less than five hundred.

So serious was the threat to Washington's position, at all events, that he called in Mercer's brigade from the extreme right of his line. Mifflin, still in his blanket coat, galloped up at the head of his Pennsylvania militiamen, who arrived in high spirits, and Doctor Rush remembered long afterward how Washington, with his aides, rode past them "in all the terrible aspect of war" and "with ardor" called on them to hurry. Rush was tending the wounded, of whom there were about twenty, and the other detail that stuck in his memory concerned a New Englander who came up to him with his right hand dangling by only a piece of skin.

This fighting was done by the leading elements only

of Cornwallis's army. When he reached the village with his main body, it was almost dark. An energetic and able commander and on the right side of forty, Cornwallis had never been inclined to underestimate Washington's ability. Sir William Erskine, his quartermaster-general, urged an immediate attack on the American position. "My Lord," said he, "if you trust those people tonight, you will see nothing of them in the morning." But the British troops had been under arms since before daylight and had been marching through the mud and fighting ever since. Grant pointed out that the Americans now lacked the means to retreat across the river: they had left their boats above Trenton. And Cornwallis decided to give his men a good night's rest and, as he said, "bag the fox" in the morning.

He has been much criticized for this decision. Wilkinson, many years after, gave his opinion that thirty minutes' fighting that evening would have meant the ruin of Washington's army. But it must be borne in mind that only a frontal attack could have been made at that hour. The roundabout march over soggy half-frozen ground, in darkness, and on a little known terrain, which would have been required in order to envelop the exposed right flank of the Americans, would have been extremely difficult, if not impossible. And a frontal attack would have involved the crossing of the creek, which most of the Hessians had found impassable in their flight a few days before, and which was now swollen afresh by the rain of the previous night. The bridge was defended by guns and by riflemen posted in the stone building of Stacy's mill close by. Three tiers of trenches fortified the slopes beyond the near-by fords; and the Americans had become famous for the perfection of their field works; and the whole position was supported by an artillery superior in numbers to the guns Cornwallis could bring against it. Cornwallis knew, of course, that more than half of Washington's army consisted of raw militiamen. But he may well have remembered that a force composed entirely of raw militiamen had killed and wounded more than a thousand of the thirty-five hundred British regulars who attacked them at Bunker Hill, and there were three times as many American muskets and six times as many American cannon here—a force, indeed, almost as numerous as the troops he had with him that night.

The British bivouacked on the hills just north of the village, building themselves great camp fires for warmth and thronging the streets in idle curiosity, after the manner of soldiers everywhere, though Knox wrote home with satisfaction that he "chucked" a few shells into the place from time to time to keep them from feeling too comfortable. All night great fires of cedar rails blazed on the entire length of the American front. To the ears of the British sentinels, who were seldom more than a hundred and fifty yards from those of their enemy, came the sound of large patrols moving along the crest above them, and the thud and scrape of picks and shovels indicated that the Americans were strengthening their works against the attack on the morrow. If the sound of rolling artillery wheels was reported to the officers of the British guard, it was attributed to the same cause. But when daylight came, the opposite side of the creek was bare. Not a gun, not a single soldier appeared above the freshly turned earth of the entrenchments, and as the sun rose, there came from far to the north the low thunder of artillery fire. Cornwallis's "fox" had stolen away.

· F I V E ·

A T eleven o'clock on that fateful night of January 2nd Washington called his general officers to a council of war at Alexander Douglass's house, St. Clair's headquarters—since his own was within range of the enemy's artillery—and asked their opinion on what had best be done. It was evident to all of them that the army was in a highly dangerous position. Its front was strong enough; the Delaware made its left flank invulnerable; but its right flank was, as the military phrase goes, "in the air." By a march of a few miles in the morning the British could turn it; in open country the militia could not be expected to sustain an attack by regular troops; and if they gave way, the whole front would probably be rolled up and the entire army trapped against the river. On the other hand, an attempt to retreat toward Philadelphia by way of Bordentown, with the enemy close behind, promised to be equally ruinous.

Somebody suggested that by a night march by the road to Sand Town and thence northwestward on the new Quaker bridge road, the army could gain Cornwallis's rear, capture Princeton at daylight, and perhaps even seize New Brunswick with its stores of food, clothing, and treasure before the day was ended. At the least the movement would extricate the army without appearing to be a retreat. At the most it might yield enormous results for the American cause throughout the country. The elements, which had so greatly hindered the offensive so far, had turned in the last few hours in

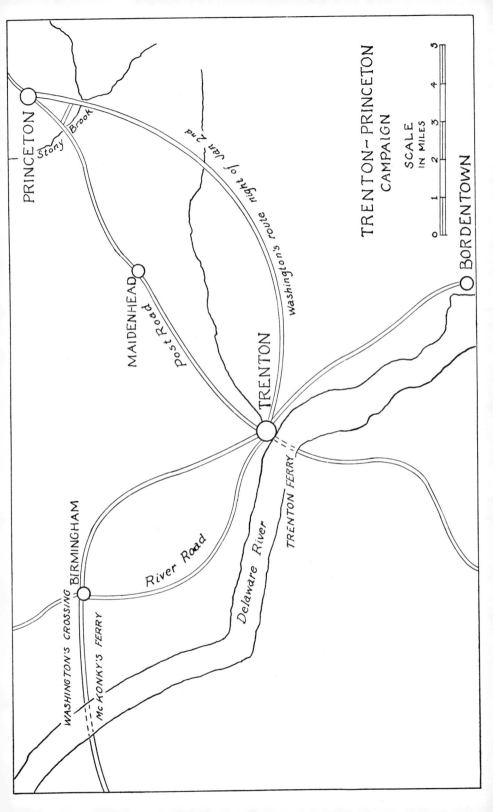

PRINCETON

Stony Brook

MAIDENHEAD

Post Road

night of Jan 2nd

washington's route

TRENTON

BIRMINGHAM

WASHINGTON'S CROSSING

McKONKY'S FERRY

River Road

Delaware River

TRENTON FERRY

BORDENTOWN

TRENTON ~ PRINCETON
CAMPAIGN

SCALE
IN MILES

0   1   2   3   4   5

its favor. The mild pleasant weather that had prevailed all day had suddenly changed. A cold wind had begun to blow from the north, and the deep mud of the roads was already freezing hard enough to bear the weight of artillery.

Some have said that Mercer suggested this movement. St. Clair claimed the credit for it. It has been thought that Washington, a stranger to that country, was not likely to have known that the proposed route existed. But in Washington's dispositions thus far: his ready adaptation of his plans to changing circumstances, the dispersal of his forces for their better provisioning in a country swept almost clean by Hessian depredations, and his concentration of them on the day, and almost at the hour, of battle there is an adumbration of the strategy of Napoleon. It is hardly conceivable that a leader capable of such planning would have placed his army in that vulnerable position at Trenton and not only awaited but invited the approach of the enemy unless he had clearly foreseen the way to profit by so doing. There can be little doubt that, whoever actually proposed the flank march at the council, the Commander-in-Chief had had it in his mind from the moment when he understood that the initiative had passed to the enemy. If he could carry this movement through successfully, he would once more be calling the tune.

There is a considerable body of evidence, moreover, to support this conclusion. Reed, Washington's adjutant general, a resident of Trenton and a former student at Princeton, must have known of the road. He had, indeed, used at least a part of it on his recent scouting expedition and had set three or four troopers of the Philadelphia light horse to patroling it the previous night, lest the British should use it in their advance, and Doctor Rush says that Reed told Washington of it. There still exists, also, a map which was drawn from information furnished by a spy, and which Cadwalader had forwarded to Washington from Crosswicks. On this map is shown the approach to the vulnerable side of the British position at Princeton, and the Quaker bridge road as the means of reaching that approach is clearly indicated.

Two men from the country near the route proposed were called into the council for their opinions of its practicability. They offered themselves as guides, and their services were accepted. The baggage train and three of the heaviest guns were sent off to Burlington by way of Bordentown under a guard commanded by General Stephen. The wheels of the rest of the artillery were wrapped in old cloth to muffle their noise on the frozen ground. Low voices passed the order to march from company to company. The troops were cautioned to preserve the utmost quietness, and at one in the morning they moved off so silently that certain officers who had slept in near-by farmhouses awoke in amazement at daylight to find them gone and had some trouble in rejoining them, since nobody below the rank of brigadier had been told of their destination. A detachment of four hundred men was left behind to keep up the fires and make a show of activity at the bridge and the fords until near dawn. But their instructions were simply to follow the army's tracks.

Easterly along the road to Sand Town (now Hamilton Avenue), by-passing that tiny hamlet and crossing Miry Run, the army traversed a tract known as the Barrens. The road, which has long since disappeared, led on to the east of Bear Swamp and joined the Quaker bridge road, by which the Friends at Crosswicks journeyed on First Days to the Stony Brook Meeting House a couple of miles south of Princeton. The Quaker bridge, about midway of the march, carried the army across the upper waters of the Assanpink. Stony Brook was crossed by the lower bridge, which stood about where it does today.

The first part of the road had been cut through dense woods, and tree stumps, which had been left here and there, brought the guns to a jolting halt from time to time and broke the wheels of some of the wagons. The horses lacked shoes, slipped and slid on the frozen ground and ice covered puddles, and had to be helped by the men. So the march was slow. In the Barrens the stubs of saplings and scrub, two to five inches in height, tripped the marching men and bruised their ill-shod feet. For the night, though cloudless, was exceedingly dark.

It was bitterly cold, too. But during the frequent halts, which were unavoidable in so long a column under such conditions, soldiers were seen "to stand, with their arms supported, fast asleep," and when they were ordered forward, they would stumble and fall heavily. It was the second night of marching for Cadwalader's and Mifflin's men; Hand's regiment and the other troops who had delayed the British march from Maidenhead had fought and marched through more than half of the previous day; and all had been under arms for many hours, strung up with the expectation of battle, and had been permitted but a few hours of rest since nightfall. Toward the rear of the column a cry that the Hessians were upon them stampeded a detachment of sleep-drugged Pennsylvanians, who did not stop their flight until they reached Burlington next morning.

According to Captain Thomas Rodney, who belonged to Mercer's brigade, his company formed a part of the advance guard, but a young captain of infantry might easily have been mistaken on such a point in the darkness of that night march. Subsequent events, taken together with the positions of the various brigades along the Assanpink the previous evening, make his statement seem unlikely. When Mercer's brigade was called in to reinforce the threatened position at the bridge, St. Clair's brigade of Sullivan's division was left on the extreme right of the American line; the army moved off by its right; and it seems improbable that any unnecessary by-passing would have been attempted in the darkness on the rough and narrow road on which the column had to be formed.

Wilkinson, moreover, whose position as St. Clair's aide should have given him a clear understanding of the order of the troops in the column, states that St. Clair's brigade was in the lead, with two six-pounders, a Massachusetts regiment forming the advance guard. Mercer's brigade appears to have followed Sullivan's division, then the Pennsylvania militia, and finally Hitchcock's New England brigade, which had been guarding the lower fords of the Assanpink and now formed the rear guard. In this way and in no other can the positions of the various brigades in the subsequent battle and the order in which they came into action be accounted for, unless one assumes that at Trenton Washington formed his advance guard of troops whom he intended to use later for a special mission and, pressed for time though he was, put himself to the trouble of forming a new advance guard at daylight next morning, when he was almost within striking distance of the enemy.

Washington had hoped to drive in the British outposts before dawn, to have captured the village and its garrison by sunrise. But here, as at Trenton just a week before, the delays of the march seemed likely to cost him the advantage of surprise. The day dawned beautifully: clear, cold, and still. Every fence-rail, every branch and twig and blade of grass was furred with hoar frost. But the head of the American column was two miles short of its objective, several hundred yards to the south of the Stony Brook Meeting House.

At that point an old back road branched off to the right across the farm of Thomas Clark. Sheltered from observation by the hill to the west of it and by the slopes beyond, it turned the corner of a wood, ran northeasterly past the Thomas Clark house and the Olden house (on what is now Olden Lane) and, crossing a ravine six or seven hundred yards south of Nassau Hall, came to the Baldwin farm (now Prospect) "at the back of Princeton," as the notes on Cadwalader's map described it. It thus turned the flank of all the British prepared defenses. The village might be entered anywhere on this side; the country had been cleared for about two miles, and there were few fences, Cadwalader had noted. And by this road Washington advanced to the attack, riding behind the Massachusetts regiment at the head of St. Clair's brigade.

In obedience to orders already issued, Mercer kept on along the main road, between Stony Brook and the hillsides to the east and north of it, toward its junction with the Princeton-Trenton post road, where the latter crossed the brook at Worth's Mill about a mile from where the back road began. He had with him what was left of Smallwood's Marylanders, the remnants of the 1st Virginia and the Delaware Continental regiments, a two-gun battery of New Jersey artillery, and perhaps some other troops, but not more than three hundred and fifty in all. His mission was to destroy the bridge in order to close that avenue of escape to the garrison of Princeton and to obstruct the British pursuit, which was sure to begin as soon as Cornwallis guessed the destination of Washington's retirement. The troops behind Mercer's brigade in the column, with a long stretch of empty road now between their van and Sullivan's rear, marched on to make the turn at the Thomas Clark farm and follow the Commander-in-Chief.

Mercer was not much more than well started on his errand, however, when Major Wilkinson, scanning the country to the westward from a point near the Quaker Meeting House, saw the beams of the rising sun flash on the bayonets of a column of enemy troops that was mounting the hill on the post road south of the bridge. It was "in the woods near Cochrane's," he remembered long afterward, and it disappeared before he could call it to the attention of Colonel Robert H. Harrison, Washington's secretary, who was riding near him. But presently he saw two horsemen leap a fence on the distant hillside, reconnoiter St. Clair's column for a minute or two, and return to the road. A few minutes later the enemy troops were seen "to come to the right about and descend the hill in quick time."

Whether Mercer on the low road beside the brook and the British on the hill beyond the bridge were aware of each other at this time is not certain. Mercer's scouts may have already pushed far enough forward to see the British hurry back across the bridge and up the road toward Princeton, and one may be sure that Washington informed Mercer of the enemy's unexpected appearance as soon as a mounted messenger could gallop across the fields and down the slope with word of it. At all events, when still some hundreds of yards southeast of the bridge, Mercer swung his column off the road, led it to the top of a knoll on his right front, and turned thence eastward to rejoin the main army. About a thousand yards ahead of him he could see St. Clair's brigade nearing the slope of the heights which have since borne Mercer's name, and it was easy to guess that toward these heights the British column must also be hastening, for they dominated the whole terrain.

A scout of the British light dragoons appeared on the nearer slope to the eastward, sighted Mercer's column, and galloped back in the direction of the post road before Mercer's riflemen could obey his order to pick the man off. So it was evident that the enemy commander would not remain long in ignorance of the American force on his right rear, and Mercer hastened his march accordingly. About four hundred yards ahead of him lay an orchard surrounded by a hedge fence. But he did not turn aside for it, and his column was in the midst of it when a volley of musketry from its northern edge brought down a shower of twigs and branches on the heads of his men.

The fifty dismounted light dragoons whom Cornwallis had left with Mawhood the previous day had raced across the little valley from the post road with orders, evidently, to bring the Americans to a stand, and the speed of their advance probably accounted for their poor shooting at so short a range. Mercer wheeled his

column into line to the left, fired a volley, charged, and
drove them back some forty or fifty yards to a point
where they had left their packs and the fall of the
ground gave them some protection from his fire. He
then made haste to line the northern edge of the orchard
with his infantry and unlimbered his two guns in the
open field on his left. For now, behind the dragoons, appeared a regiment of British infantry in line of battle,
with two cannon on their right and, in front of them,
Colonel Mawhood, their commander, riding a brown
pony with the negligence of an English gentleman out
to view his estate on a frosty morning, while a couple of
spaniels yapped and frisked about him.

CHAPTER IV

"A Fine Fox Chase, Boys!"

· O N E ·

THAT map which Cadwalader sent to Washington from Crosswicks bears clear evidence of the state of nerves that prevailed among the British forces at Princeton during the first four or five days after the Hessian defeat at Trenton. They had an outpost of a hundred men at the bridge at Worth's Mill and a chain of sentinels reaching to the top of the hill beyond it. A support, with two small cannon, guarded the road at a point about halfway between the bridge and the village. There was a battery of eight six-pounders at the head of what is now Nassau Street, with breastworks of fascines in the fields on either flank. In the road, directly in front of the college, two small guns were placed so as to sweep the length of the present Witherspoon Street, which was the route to Rocky Hill. A couple of hundred yards to the eastward three or four pieces commanded the approach from Kingston, and on the morning when the spy left for Crosswicks a hundred men had begun a fortification on the higher ground near an orchard to the north, apparently not far from the end of the present Vandeventer Avenue.

But the arrival of the troops under Grant and Cornwallis had dispelled the fears that had inspired these precautions. When Mawhood marched off for Trenton soon after daybreak on the 3rd of January, it seemed certain that, with the main army facing Washington at Trenton, the only danger to be apprehended was from some roving band of militia. Against an attack by such

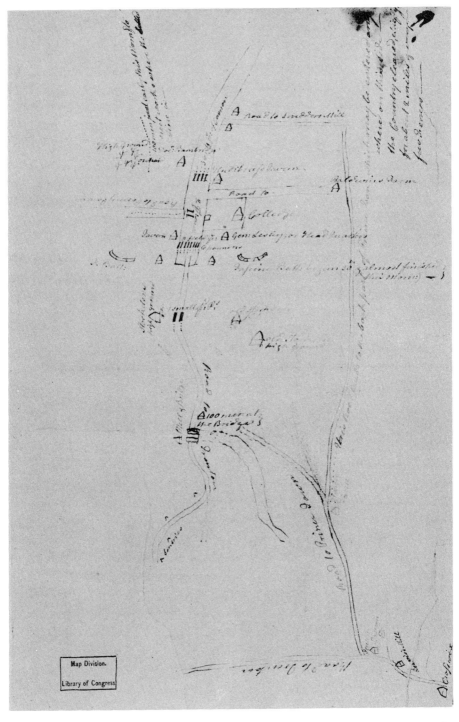

The "spy" map of Princeton which Cadwalader sent Washington Dec. 31, 1776.
It was drawn by Cadwalader in Crosswicks from information furnished him by
a young spy.

troops, the 40th regiment of Foot, which Mawhood left behind him, was more than ample. The feeling of security at Princeton had, indeed, become so strong that on the previous night the patrol in the direction of Allentown had been discontinued. This was a stroke of great good luck for Washington. Otherwise his approach must surely have been discovered, and he would have been committed to a stand-up fight against the entire Fourth Brigade assembled under arms and in the best possible position to resist him. He would probably have been victorious, since he would have outnumbered the British more than three to one, but the battle would have cost him far more time and greater losses than he could well afford.

Mawhood had with him the fifty dismounted dragoons, the 17th and the 55th infantry regiments and two guns. But the greater part of the 55th was somewhere between a half mile and a mile behind him, when his mounted scouts on the hillside beyond the bridge sighted St. Clair's brigade near the Quaker Meeting House. Mawhood's first thought appears to have been that Cornwallis had routed Washington's army the previous afternoon, and that these troops were some fleeing fragment of it. But they were evidently numerous enough to be a threat to the supplies at Princeton, since only the 40th remained there, and in any case they ought to be destroyed.

By one of his mounted men, who went galloping back to the village to give the alarm, he sent orders to the 55th to return and join the 40th in opposing the enemy's advance. With the troops under his immediate control he descended the hill in quick time—the movement of which Wilkinson saw the beginning—recrossed the

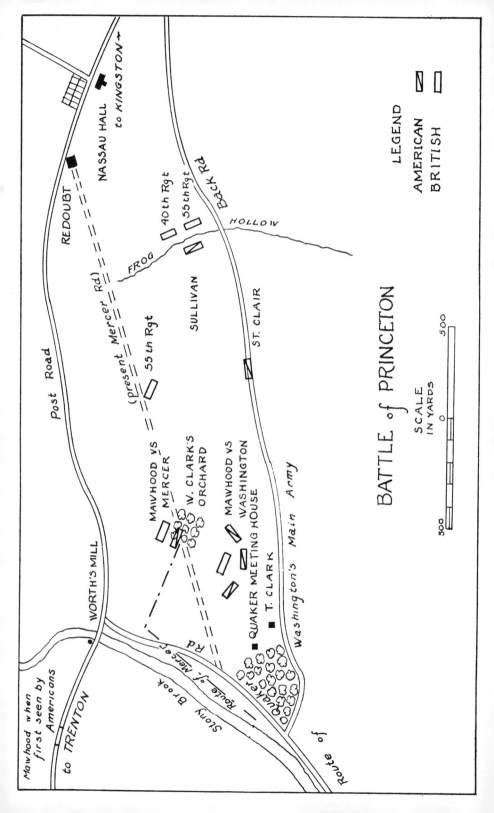

BATTLE of PRINCETON

SCALE IN YARDS

500   0   500

LEGEND

AMERICAN   BRITISH

to KINGSTON →

NASSAU HALL

REDOUBT

Post Road

(present Mercer Rd)

FROG   HOLLOW

Back Rd

40th Rgt

55th Rgt

55th Rgt

SULLIVAN

ST. CLAIR

MAWHOOD vs MERCER

W. CLARK'S ORCHARD

MAWHOOD vs WASHINGTON

QUAKER MEETING HOUSE

T. CLARK

Washington's Main Army

WORTH'S MILL

Mawhood when first seen by Americans

to TRENTON

Stony Brook

Route of Mercer Rd

Route of Quaker

bridge and, at a point where the road angled to the
north, he left it for a direct line cross-country toward
Mercer Heights as the shortest route by which he could
rejoin the rest of his brigade. But now one of his mounted scouts rode in from the eastward with the information that another rebel force was close at hand, hardly
six hundred yards to his right and rear and pressing
swiftly toward the enemy troops he had already seen.

In these circumstances should he continue his march
and reunite his forces before giving battle, or would it
not be better to destroy this isolated detachment while
he had the opportunity to do so? It should not take him
long. The scout's report indicated that the enemy's
strength was slightly less than his own. In guns the
two forces were evenly matched. It would be strange if
British regulars, who were, moreover, fresh and recently
well fed, could not conquer these already once defeated
rebels, who must have been marching most of the night,
and probably on empty bellies.

There was a small wooden house belonging to Thomas
Olden where Mawhood paused to make this decision.
(The building has since been moved some three hundred
yards to the northward of where it stood in 1777.) One
of its occupants, an old man of eighty-five, wrote afterwards what he called "A Brief Narrative" of what followed. But his name is unknown, and his manuscript
has been generally called the Thomas Olden Diary, although he was evidently a much older man than Thomas
Olden was. In his dooryard he and the women of his
household and a neighbor woman stood, watching, while
a part of Mawhood's men piled their knapsacks in a
corner of his field and the regiment formed and advanced, with the dragoons racing ahead to ambush the

American column at the orchard's northern edge, which was clearly visible only about four hundred yards across the little valley to the eastward of the house. But when the volleys crashed and the cannon began to boom, the whine of spent bullets and the thud of round shot near-by drove the watchers to the cellar for safety.

Ensconced in their turn behind the hedge from which they had driven the dragoons, Mercer's men greeted the appearance of the British battle line with a volley. But they were hungry and very tired, and many of them 'were armed with rifles, which took more time to load than muskets because of the necessity of wrapping the bullet in a greased patch of cloth to make it respond to the grooving of the bore. They are credited with getting off three volleys in all, one of which must have been the one they fired at the dragoons. Wilkinson, watching from a point near the Olden house on the southern slope of Mercer Heights, saw the powder smoke mount into the wintry sunshine "in one beautiful cloud." But, though the range was only forty yards and they loaded their muskets, according to their custom, with two or three buckshot as well as a bullet, they seem to have done little damage. Mawhood halted to fire only once, then led his men in a bayonet charge that broke the American line and swept its fragments back through the orchard trees and out across the hedge on the southern side.

A sergeant remembered afterwards how Mercer gave the command: " 'Retreat,' in tones of distress." Then it was every man for himself, and death for all but the swift, even for many of the wounded. There seems to have been a killer spirit abroad among Mawhood's men that morning. A lieutenant, who had dragged his broken leg to the shelter of a wagon in William Clark's near-by farmyard, was sought out and killed with bayonets. Lieutenant Bartholomew Yeates, shot and clubbed, was stabbed thirteen times, though he begged for quarter. He lived long enough after the battle to make an affidavit of these facts, and Doctor Rush attested it. And these were only two of several instances of equal barbarity. A few days later Washington, acting in the spirit of the times, sent to Howe a protest against this brutal behavior and accompanied his complaint with the statement of the dying Yeates.

Less reprehensible was the killing of Mercer, for he went down fighting. About fifty yards from William Clark's barn, which stood near the southwest corner of the orchard, Mercer on foot—a bullet had broken a foreleg of his splendid gray charger—strove, sword in hand, to rally his men. But only a few of them had bayonets, and to all of them it appeared that the day was lost. For the rest of the army, which they had expected to find coming up from the road to the southward to support them, was nowhere to be seen. Only Sullivan's troops were visible, and they were too far away to be of any assistance. Another moment and Mercer was surrounded by enemy soldiers. A surtout, which concealed his insignia of rank, caused them to think they had Washington at their mercy. "Call for quarters, you damn rebel," one of them shouted. But Mercer's Scottish blood boiled at the insult. He struck out with his sword till a gun butt brought him to his knees, and, bleeding from seven bayonet wounds, he feigned death in order to escape further injuries.

Not far away, Captain John Fleming, who headed what was left of the 1st Virginia regiment that day, managed to get a few of his men into formation. "Gentlemen, dress the line before you make ready," he commanded in an effort to steady them. "We will dress you," a British soldier yelled at him, and a moment later Fleming fell dead.

Colonel Haslet of the Delaware regiment dropped with a bullet through his brain. At the crossing of the river on Christmas night he had fallen into the icy waters of the river, and his legs had swelled severely, but he had gone into this action on foot. In his pocket was an order detaching him on recruiting service, but he had said nothing about it, lest it keep him out of the fighting.

Captain Neil of the New Jersey artillery, who had managed to loose a few rounds that did some execution on Mawhood's right wing, fell fighting in defense of his guns. The British seized them, swung them around, and opened fire with them and their own two guns on the Americans, who were now in full flight toward a strip of woods about half a mile to the southward. The light infantry chased the fugitives down the slope to a fence from which the ground rose gradually to the house of Thomas Clark (still standing) some five hundred yards south of the southern edge of the orchard.

The rest of Mawhood's men were following. But suddenly the appearance of new and unexpected enemies brought them to a halt. The light infantrymen swiftly deployed along the fence and opened fire. Mawhood reformed his line of battle, brought up his guns, and put them in action near a solitary oak tree on a knoll on his right. For the head of a strong column of American infantry had appeared over the crest a little to the westward of the Thomas Clark house, and a battery of artillery unlimbered for action between some haystacks and the eastern end of the house.

The new arrivals were Moulder's battery and Cadwalader's brigade of Pennsylvania militia, who had reached a point on the road to the east of the farmhouse a few moments before. Greene had wheeled them to their left and sent them hurrying up the slope. What followed took so short a time that it seems hardly credible to modern readers—some fifteen minutes, according to the watches of officers engaged in the action. So small was the battlefield, so few the combatants.

As soon as the Pennsylvanians had passed the farmhouse, Cadwalader attempted to form them in line by swinging alternate squads of eight men each—platoons was the word for them at that day—to the right and left. But the sight that met their eyes was too much for the courage of the half-trained militiamen. The broken remnants of Mercer's brigade were streaming toward them, hotly pursued by the victorious foe. The opposite slope was dotted with dead or writhing compatriots. The British guns blazed, and although they fired too high, their shot and shell screamed horridly overhead. It would have strained the nerves of well drilled troops to change from column into line under such conditions. The Pennsylvanians broke, bolted, and, mingling with Mercer's fleeing men, ran for the shelter of the slope they had just ascended.

This should have been the moment for Mawhood to charge. But Moulder's gunners were made of sterner stuff than their comrades in the infantry. Their two long four-pounders opened with grape shot on the light infantrymen at the fence and stopped the dragoons, who had begun to work around the American right. Captain

Rodney, with thirty or forty of his own men, a few of the boldest of Mercer's, and a detachment of Pennsylvanians, took position among the haystacks to the right of the guns and, under a galling fire of musketry, checked a dash for the battery by the enemy in front until help could arrive from the north, as soon it did.

If any of the combatants had time to glance in that direction, they saw a big man on a tall white horse galloping down the road from Sullivan's division with a little group of aides and orderlies pelting behind him. It was Washington and his staff. Behind him came at a run the battle-tried 7th Virginia Continentals, and behind them Hand's regiment of riflemen.

Washington rode among the broken Pennsylvanians and Mercer's men on the slope behind the house. He had seen British regulars stampeded by inferior numbers of French and Indians in the backwoods near Fort Duquesne twenty years before and was not disposed to be contemptuous of these panic-stricken novices, hungry and well-nigh exhausted as they were. He knew them to be fundamentally courageous, and he told them so.

"Parade with us, my brave fellows!" he shouted. "There is but a handful of the enemy, and we will have them directly."

They rallied and formed. Mercer's men flocked to join them. Hat in hand, Washington waved them forward, rode ahead of them to within thirty paces of the British line, and there, between the two fires, halted. His action may well have recalled to some who saw it that shameful morning at Kipp's Bay the previous September, when he had sat his horse alone, facing the fire of the British advance, as if courting death, and not one man of the frightened troops scuttling past on the road behind him was moved by his example to stand and fight by his side. What a difference today! Cadwalader's men deployed and stood firm. Mifflin's brigade came up on their right.

As simultaneous volleys crashed from friend and foe, young Irish John Fitzgerald, Washington's aide, pulled his hat over his eyes rather than see his chieftain fall, as he felt sure he must. But when he looked again, he saw Washington still in the saddle, unharmed, and still waving the lines forward, and heard his calm tones ordering: "Bring up the troops, Colonel Fitzgerald. The day is our own."

The rear guard of the army had come up by this time—the veteran New Englanders, with Hitchcock still leading them, though his disease was to kill him ten days later. Washington sent them into action around the eastern end of the hill against Mawhood's left. A hundred men of the Pennsylvania militia under Captain Henry had outflanked and driven the light infantry from the fence. Beyond them Hand's riflemen had the left flank of the British battle line under a deadly fire. The New Englanders advanced like the seasoned troops they were, formed line at two hundred yards from the enemy as if on parade. At a hundred yards they halted and fired a volley, reloaded, advanced again, firing by platoons, and finally charged.

All along the line the fire of the Americans was, as it always was, says Trevelyan, "extraordinarily destructive, whenever they held their ground." Under the salvos of grape from Moulder's guns the enemy were mown down, it was said, "in rows": their wounded could be heard screaming. The attack was timed to perfection. As the New Englanders charged, the Pennsylvanians charged also. The enemy left wing was enveloped; the guns on the right were taken, though their captain and eight men died to defend them. The British, greatly outnumbered though they were, fought grimly. Washington exclaimed in admiration of their disciplined courage and wished aloud for a day when he might have men with the colors long enough to make such soldiers of them.

Nevertheless it was now Mawhood's turn to give the order to retreat. His men cut their way out with the bayonet, broke ranks to flee, re-formed, were again broken, and ran at last in wild disorder back to the post road and down the post road toward the bridge, leaving almost a quarter of their strength dead or wounded on the field.

The victors raced after them. Washington, giving free rein to his elation, galloped with the pursuit, shouting: "It's a fine fox chase, my boys!" He joined the crowd of soldiers who paused, breathless, thirsty, and laughing, in the dooryard of the house near which Mawhood's men had piled their knapsacks only three-quarters of an hour before. There was "not a man among them but showed joy in his countenance," wrote the anonymous author of the "Olden Diary."

The fifty British dragoons—fifty no longer, it must be supposed, for they were in the fighting from first to last—made a stand above the bridge to cover their comrades' retreat. But they were quickly dislodged, and the whole rout streamed away, the foremost up the hill toward Maidenhead, while Hand's riflemen hunted the rest for four miles along the valley of the brook in the direction of Pennington, taking many prisoners and shooting those who resisted. So long was the chase that many of the pursuers could rejoin the army only at Pluckemin next day. For Cornwallis's troops were again in Princeton when they sought to return.

· T W O ·

DURING those crowded forty-five minutes—the whole battle, from the dragoons' ambush at the orchard to the routing of Mawhood's force in front of the Thomas Clark house, actually appears to have taken no longer—the British 55th regiment remained inactive in a small wood on Mercer Heights, which they had reached when the fighting began. Had they marched to Mawhood's assistance they must have exposed their flank to St. Clair's brigade, which had halted below the Olden house to the east of them. A move toward the fighting by St. Clair would have exposed his flank to an attack by the 55th. Neither force knew the strength of the other. So they remained where they were, each containing the other, until the action ended.

At sight of the defeat and rout of the 17th, which swept with it their brigade commander, the 55th proceeded to carry out the last order they had received from him and returned swiftly toward Princeton. They formed on the left of the 40th, which had marched out from the village and occupied the ridge whose crest slopes gradually from the present site of the Presbyterian Theological Seminary to that of the Princeton Inn. The position was an advantageous one. The brook that drains what was locally known as Frog Hollow ran across its front, as that brook, channelled for the exasperation of golfers, does today. Beyond the brook the ground rose, probably more abruptly than now, to the present site of the Graduate College and formed a ravine that presented a considerable obstacle to troops advancing from the south. The 55th had only about half a mile to retire in order to reach this locality, and the corresponding movement by St. Clair and the rest of Sullivan's division, which continued to follow the road, must have taken enough longer to give the two British regiments ample time to organize their defense.

In numbers the 40th and 55th together were almost equal to the force that was about to attack them; they had just seen what British discipline could do against enormous odds; but they had also seen the 17th destroyed in spite of that discipline; and they knew that it was only a matter of time before Mawhood's vanquishers would be added to their more immediate assailants. At all events, the stand they made was of the briefest. When a couple of American regiments scaled the slope unseen and appeared suddenly within sixty paces of them, they fled in panic. This was "owing to the manner of the attack," Sullivan wrote afterwards, but he did not explain what that manner was. From the nature of the ground it seems probable that it was a turning movement around the British left flank, which would have threatened their line of retreat to the village and to the only roads to safety.

Some of the fugitives gained the road down what is now Witherspoon Street and made good their escape to Rocky Hill, whence they could reach New Brunswick by a circuitous route. Many, pressed closely by Sullivan's troops, sought refuge in Nassau Hall, knocked out the few panes of glass that had outlasted the occupation of the building by both American and British soldiers, and opened fire from the windows. But Hamilton brought up his guns and sent a cannon shot through the wall of the prayer hall, decapitating the portrait of King George II, which hung within. Another shot caromed off the masonry and came close to killing Major Wilkinson's horse, as he recorded indignantly some forty years later. Captain James Moore, a resident of Princeton whose property had been mercilessly plundered, led a rush against the door and broke it in. A white flag appeared at one of the windows, and the garrison—"a haughty crabbed set of men," as one American sergeant observed them—filed out and gave up their arms. Several British sick and wounded were placed on parole, and a number of American soldiers, who had been held prisoner in the building, were liberated.

The victors devoted the next two hours to assembling their widely scattered troops, collecting the wounded— they lacked the time to bury the dead—and disposing of the booty. Washington estimated the British losses at four hundred, of whom ninety-six enlisted men and four officers were dead, and three hundred, including fourteen officers, were prisoners. Howe, who had every motive for minimizing the defeat, admitted that seventy-six of Mawhood's command were killed or wounded, and that a hundred and eighty-seven were missing: a total of two hundred and sixty-three. But the fact remained that the British crack Fourth Brigade had been practically annihilated at a cost to the American army of thirty enlisted men and fourteen officers killed. Of the wounded on both sides, however, most died: their injuries, on account of the close, fierce nature of the combat, proving fatal.

But if the victory was cheap in numbers, it was dear in quality, and doubly so since officers of ability were

rare in the American army at that time. Mercer, who
died after nine days of lingering agony, was irreplace-
able, and the list included some of the best and bravest:
Colonels Haslet and Porter, Captains Neil and Fleming, and Captain William Shippin of the Pennsylvania
marines among their number.

The Americans, according to their own accounts,
showed the same magnanimity that distinguished them
at Trenton, treated the wounded with a humanity that
is amazing, considering the cruelty with which they had
just seen the enemy deal with Mercer's men. "You are
safe enough, we are after live men," they assured those
who begged for quarter, and they shared with them the
whisky in their canteens, if they were lucky enough to
have any. Some of the wounded were cared for in the
house beside the post road, twenty in William Clark's
house, several at Thomas Clark's, whither Mercer was
carried, and at least sixty were taken in wagons to
Princeton.

Arriving soon after the battle, Doctor Rush found
the field still literally red with blood, which had collected in pools on the frozen ground. In the Thomas
Clark house a British surgeon's mate was caring for
Mercer and a Captain McPherson of the 17th, who had
been shot through the lungs but eventually recovered—
"in consequence of the loss of a hundred and forty
ounces of blood," according to Rush. Rush immediately
set about his grim work of mercy, ordering leg ampu-
tations on four British soldiers, all of whom survived.

He did the little he could for Captain the Honorable
William Leslie of the 17th, nephew of General Alexander Leslie and son of the Scottish Earl of Levin,
whom he found desperately wounded on the field. When

Rush was a medical student at Edinburgh the Earl had shown him much kindness, but the poor young Captain was beyond all hope. Among the prisoners were some of his men, by whom he was beloved. They begged to be permitted to take him with them in a wagon, when they were marched away, and Rush granted their request. Leslie died at Pluckemin the following morning and was buried with military honors in the village graveyard there next day.

At Princeton, officers who had leisure to do so, gathered at what Major Wilkinson describes as "the provost's house," President Witherspoon's Tusculum, where, though they were anxious about Washington, whom they had not seen since he galloped away in pursuit of Mawhood's men, they made an excellent meal of the breakfast that had been prepared for the officers of the 40th.

Soldiers, gloriously idle for the time being, wandered about the village, admiring the brick houses, which they thought "elegant," and "especially," as one of them wrote in his diary, "the College which has 52 rooms in it, but the whole town . . . ravaged and ruined by the enemy." They amused themselves by counting the bullet holes in their clothing. A sergeant of long service for that army observed that whereas he had fortified his courage at the Battle of Long Island with draughts of rum mixed with gunpowder, he had felt just as brave here without any stimulant. He discovered with amazement that the end of one of his forefingers had been shot off without his knowing it. Bullets had cut the straps from his pack, and he had lost it. He replaced it with the well furnished knapsack of a British officer.

As for the booty, Washington made light of it in his

report to the President of the Congress. "We took two brass field pieces," he wrote, "but for want of horses, could not bring them away, we also took some blankets, shoes, and a few other trifling articles, burned the hay" —which was, of course, tantamount to the destruction of the gasoline and oil dumps of a present day army— "and destroyed such other things, as the shortness of the time would admit." Captain Rodney remembered the battlefield as strewn with "baggage." But by this he can only have meant the knapsacks dropped by the men of the 17th in their flight. If Mawhood actually had any baggage train with him that morning, which seems improbable, he would certainly not have allowed it to leave the road.

Knox, however, wrote home that "a considerable quantity of military stores, blankets and guns, etc." were captured. In writing about the victory to Silas Deane at Paris, Robert Morris listed baggage and other stores, a hundred oxen and a number of sheep among the spoil, and it appears that a good many valuable horses were taken. It has been suggested that Washington purposely belittled the amount of the booty, lest the Congress think that the wants of his soldiers had thereby been satisfied.

For all that had to be done, the time, as Washington stated, was, indeed, short. Two hours had hardly passed before Leslie's brigade from Maidenhead, with the rest of Cornwallis's army strung out on the Trenton road behind them, reached the hilltop above the bridge over Stony Brook. "This they did," Knox wrote to his wife, "in a most infernal sweat—running, puffing and blowing and swearing at being so outwitted." Below them they could see only a detachment of the Northumberland County, Pennsylvania, militia, under the command of Major John Kelly, working furiously to carry out an order from Washington for the destruction of the bridge, and beyond the working party, Forrest's battery ready to open fire.

But the British had heard all about the defeat of the early morning from those fugitives who had gained the Maidenhead road, and Cornwallis's already healthy respect for Washington's generalship had been considerably strengthened by the events of the last twenty-four hours. Taking no chances of being caught in the narrow defile in front of him by fire from the high ground beyond, he halted, unlimbered some of his guns and opened fire. Forrest answered, but the British cannonade was so heavy that the working party had to flee, though not before their commander was hurled into the stream by the end of a plank which was struck by a cannon ball.

Forrest, his mission accomplished, withdrew. Only the stringers of the bridge remained, and the British infantry, who were now ordered to advance, had to wade breastdeep through the icy water, while others salvaged and replaced the planks for the artillery to cross. The march had no sooner been resumed, however, than there came another delay. A cannon boomed from the nearer side of the village, and the ball of a thirty-two pounder whirred overhead. It was one of the guns in the fortifications which the British had built in their alarm during the previous week. A few stragglers had touched it off at random. But Cornwallis, no doubt well-informed of the location of those works and realizing that they would make an excellent support for a rear-guard action like that of the previous day, if Washington should choose to fight one, halted his column again and made a strong and elaborate reconnaissance.

This brought him word of the British dead strewing the battlefield, of the improvised hospitals in the neighboring houses, of the spiked guns behind the fascine breastworks, and of one of Mawhood's brass pieces spiked and left where it stood. Procter had taken the other, leaving one of his inferior iron guns behind him. But no enemies in arms were discovered. Meanwhile valuable time was slipping away. It was noon when the British vanguard entered the village, and the last of the American army was filing off toward Kingston through the eastern outskirts.

The British light troops and a mounted detachment of dragoons pressed forward swiftly in pursuit. What with the herds of sheep and oxen, the prisoners, and the baggage wagons laden with the spoil, the American column could move but slowly. Moulder, who was with the rear guard had to unlimber his guns and open fire to cover the retreat, and when he wished to withdraw, the enemy musket balls flew so thick that he dared not bring up his teams to do so. His men ran the guns up the road by the prolonges, forty men on each rope. They were "no grass combers," they said, to spike them and leave them to the enemy, as their captain had Washington's instructions to do in case of need.

Even so, the guns might have been lost, and the men as well. For the dragoons rode after them and only halted when the Philadelphia light horsemen—twenty-two in number—lined up across the road, ready at the word of command from their captain, "Quaker Sam" Morris, to charge. At Morristown a few days later Moulder was brought before a court of inquiry for thus exposing his men. He was exonerated, but the proceeding makes it clear that gunners like his were more precious than their guns in the sight of their commander-in-chief.

Kingston was reached without further fighting, and the bridge over the Millstone River was destroyed as soon as the last of the troops had passed over it. Ahead lay New Brunswick, with its quantities of military stores, large stocks of food, shoes, and clothing, and seventy thousand pounds in golden guineas. The blow of such a capture might end the war. The acquisition of so great a sum in hard money would, in any event, do wonders for the waning credit of the patriot government. Before leaving Princeton, or somewhere on the road, or at Kingston—accounts differ—Washington gathered his generals around him on horseback to help him decide whether he should press on and attempt to seize the place before Cornwallis could overtake him, or turn aside and seek safety in the hills to the northward.

The chance was tempting. He had hoped to be able to take it. But New Brunswick was eighteen miles away. His men had already marched as far as that since midnight—the second night march in succession for half of them. They had fought a battle—the second combat in the past twenty-four hours for many of them. And some of them had been under arms for forty hours, with only the briefest periods of rest. If he had possessed eight hundred, or even six hundred, fresh men, he wrote Hancock, he would have marched on. But it was Trenton over again, and this time he had Cornwallis's whole army almost on his heels. It seemed probable, moreover, that Howe had arrived at New Brunswick with fresh troops from New York. For Washington to be caught, with his well-nigh exhausted troops, between that force and Cornwallis's army would have meant ruin. So, at Kingston, he turned regretfully to the left and took the road to Somerset Court House (now Millstone), with Morristown, by way of Pluckemin, as his destination.

There was no sign of any pursuit by the enemy, only a strong party of light horse, which took the road on the west bank of the Millstone and reached Rocky Hill about the time the American vanguard crowned the heights on the opposite side of the stream. Their mission was probably one of observation only. But on sighting them Washington sent Captain Rodney, with a picked force of carpenters, to destroy the bridge at that point, which was done before the enemy horsemen reached it.

Night fell. But the American soldiers, who had left Princeton in high spirits, continued to plod doggedly forward, though this march brought the total distance they had tramped since midnight up to more than thirty miles. It was eleven o'clock and bitterly cold when they stumbled into the little village of Somerset Court House. The prisoners were locked up in the court house building. Their captors, less fortunate, either dropped in their tracks on the frozen ground and slept the sleep of the utterly exhausted or clustered about huge fires, on which they piled the rails from the neighboring fences and every other piece of loose timber they could lay their hands on. The Pennsylvania militia were especially wretched. For some misguided officer at Trenton the previous night had ordered them to load their blankets on their baggage wagons, apparently in ignorance that the baggage train was not to accompany the troops.

At Somerset Court House it was learned that the army had arrived only a little too late to capture a Brit-

ish train of twenty wagons laden with linen and clothing and escorted by only a hundred men, which four
hundred New Jersey militia had allowed to escape on its
march from Hillsboro to New Brunswick. But there
must have been few of Washington's men who were not
too weary to feel any great chagrin at this occurrence.

The failure to capture a few baggage wagons can
hardly have diminished their satisfaction in their
achievements of the past ten days. Ill-fed, half-clad,
lacking shoes, poorly armed, and half of them raw militia, they had destroyed two of the best brigades the
King could send against them. They had brought to a
stand at Trenton the previous night a British army
equal in strength to their own and superior to theirs in
everything else but their spirit of dogged determination.
They had outmarched and outmaneuvered their enemy,
defeated him in detail, and threatened his base of supplies so seriously that he had ceased to pursue them and
was, at this very hour, pressing on through the night to
save it from the possibility of capture.

Four long years and nine months later, at a dinner
that followed the capitulation of the British at York-
town, Cornwallis rose to respond to a toast and, good
English sportsman that he was, lauded his vanquisher's
generalship in this campaign. "When the illustrious
part that your Excellency has borne in this long and
arduous contest becomes a matter of history," he said,
"fame will gather your brightest laurels rather from
the banks of the Delaware than from those of the
Chesapeake." In Prussia, Dietrich Heinrich von Bülow,
whose studies of the art of war won him the name of
"the father of modern tactics," wrote of the attack on

Trenton that it was "one of the best planned and most ably executed" military movements of the century. "It was, however," he continued, "excelled by the Princeton offensive, and both operations are sufficient to elevate a general to the temple of immortality."

CHAPTER V

"These Feats Have Turned the Scale"

· O N E ·

OWING to the haste with which Cornwallis had marched toward the sound of the guns at Princeton, his troops had moved with more speed than cohesion. It was late in the afternoon when the last of them entered the village and he could proceed to follow Washington with the well organized and compact column which the situation required. The repair of the bridge at Kingston delayed him still further. By that time, of course, he had learned of Washington's swing toward Somerset Court House. But the great stores of supplies and the military chest at New Brunswick, rather than the pursuit of the American army, had now become his chief concern, and he pressed on with all speed to protect them. For he could not be sure that his wily adversary might not attempt to fool him again by wheeling on to the cross road that ran eastward from Rocky Hill and, by a march of only about three miles, get back on the main road ahead of him.

Only less weary than the Americans—and not, like them, sustained by the joy of victory—the British soldiers pushed on through the night. At Princeton they had viewed the dismal evidence of Mawhood's defeat; they had had "nothing to eat for two days," according to one of their young officers; and there was no blessed halt for them at eleven. Day was dawning when their vanguard reached their destination. It was nine o'clock before the last of them limped in.

At New Brunswick they found that the garrison had

been greatly alarmed. Fugitives from the 40th and 55th regiments, certain that the enemy was hot on their heels, had brought word of the débâcle at Princeton soon after noon of the previous day. Howe, characteristically enough, had not arrived at New Brunswick, and the only reinforcement had been the 46th Foot, which was not enough, in the judgment of General Matthew, the commander of the post, to enable him to defend it adequately. Commandeering all the wagons he could lay his hands on, he loaded them with as much of the stores and supplies as they could carry and sent them, together with the military chest and his distinguished prisoner, General Lee, under a strong escort, to the bridge a couple of miles up the Raritan to seek safety on the farther bank. His troops he had formed on the heights outside the town and there awaited the enemy until word of the approach of Cornwallis put an end to his anxieties.

Four days later, Cornwallis wrote to Lord George Germain from New Brunswick that the injury done to the British cause by the recent operations of the Americans had been repaired. "That is now done and all is safe," he assured him. Washington, to be sure, was at Morristown by that time, "with about seven thousand men," according to the British intelligence service. But Cornwallis wrote: "He cannot subsist long where he is. I should imagine that he means to repass the Delaware at Alexandria. The season of the year will make it difficult for us to follow him, but the march alone will destroy his army."

The British in New York were equally complacent. They masked the news of the destruction of Mawhood's brigade with lavish praise of the valor of the 17th Foot.

On the day on which Cornwallis wrote to Germain, Howe publicly thanked Colonel Mawhood, the officers and soldiers of the 17th, and the other detachments "for their Gallantry and good Conduct in the Attack made upon the Enemy on the 3rd Instant." *The New York Gazette and Weekly Mercury* of January 13th described the battle as a brilliant British victory and placed the American loss at four hundred in an account of it that moved the *Pennsylvania Journal* to ask: "Who is the greatest liar upon earth?" and to answer: "Hugh Gaine of New York, printer." An aide of Clinton's wrote him from New York that Mawhood would have taken the whole American army, if his other two regiments had supported the 17th. But the writer had the good sense to add that Washington's escape from Trenton was "a fatal oversight." Ambrose Serle, Lord Howe's secretary, recorded in his diary a "skirmish in the Jersies," in which the American losses were much greater than the British, and even Stedman, who should have known better, since he wrote twenty years after the event, adds a similar statement about the losses to his praise of the performance of the 17th at Princeton, which he calls "one of the most gallant exploits of the whole war."

Rall and the Hessians at Trenton were made the whipping boys for the entire fiasco, and as little as possible was said of Washington's extrication of his army from behind the Assanpink and the American victory at Princeton. Only poor von Heister took what comfort he could from the latter. In a letter to his prince on the fifth of January he wrote: "Just now I receive the report that an English brigade has shared the same fate as the Rall brigade. . . . The English regiments have no flags or cannon with them and so are saved the misfortune of losing them." He was mistaken, of course, about the cannon.

Howe, who had never intended to fight a winter campaign and had been involved in this one only through those "rather too large links" in his chain of posts across the Jerseys, had no desire to spoil a pleasant sojourn in New York by engaging in another. "The enemy moves with so much more celerity than we possibly can," he wrote to Germain in explanation of his inactivity, and laid the blame for the slow marching of his troops on the heavy baggage trains required by the Hessians.

To make sure of not being disturbed, he concentrated the British forces in New Jersey at Perth Amboy and New Brunswick—five thousand at each post—and devoted himself to arrangements for his investiture with the Order of Knight Commander of the Bath. This took place on the 18th and was celebrated with a ball and an elaborate supper, fireworks, skating and sleighing parties, and dancing in the streets, for which both soldiers and sailors were given special liberty.

The bold appearance of a strong American force in front of Kingsbridge on the Harlem River that same day gave Howe no concern. He knew that New York was safe from any attack and that his posts in New Jersey were too strong to be assailed successfully by any force that Washington was able to bring against them, and he felt confident that a campaign in the coming summer would easily regain all that he had recently lost. It had to be admitted, however, that the campaign had certain regrettable consequences. Serle set down in his diary on the 9th the opinion that the "idle affair at Trenton on Xmas day" would probably stimulate the raising of rebel troops in Connecticut. And two days after the festivities of the investiture, Howe himself wrote to Germain, "with much concern," that the enemy's successes had "thrown us further back than was at first apprehended, from the great encouragement it has given the rebels."

Up among the snow covered hills at Morristown, Washington would have stated the matter even more strongly.

· T W O ·

WASHINGTON had halted only for the night at Somerset Court House and had moved on to Pluckemin on January 4th. There he remained for a day in order to rest his men and horses and to await the return of stragglers and others who had been separated from their organizations by the accidents of march and combat. About a thousand of these, including many of Hand's riflemen, whom Cornwallis's arrival had prevented from returning to Princeton after their pursuit of Mawhood's men, rejoined him here, and a few more came in at Morristown, where the army arrived on the 6th.

Although he had been disappointed in his hope of taking New Brunswick, Washington was delighted, and with good reason, with the success he had achieved. In ordering Putnam to move his command to Crosswicks he wrote on the 5th that the British appeared to be "panic-struck," and that he had "some hopes of driving them out of the Jerseys." The same day he directed Heath, who was to be reinforced by four thousand militia from New England, to threaten New York. The enemy were "in great consternation," Washington told him, and Heath's offensive might force them to withdraw troops from New Jersey. Two days later Washington forwarded to Heath a report that there were so few troops left in New York that it might be possible to capture the city.

This proved to be untrue. But the optimism of the Commander-in-Chief was shared by his generals. From Morristown, Knox wrote to his wife: "The enemy were within nineteen miles of Philadelphia, they are now sixty miles. We have driven them from almost the whole of West Jersey. The panic is still kept up. . . . They have sent their baggage to Staten Island from the Jerseys, and we are very well informed they are doing the same from New York . . . 'there is a tide in the affairs of men, which taken at the flood leads on to victory.' " Greene wrote to Thomas Paine on the 9th: "The two late actions at Trenton and Princeton have put a very different face upon affairs. Within a fortnight past we have taken and killed of Howe's army between two and three thousand men—Our loss is trifling—we are daily picking up their parties—yesterday we took seventy prisoners and thirty loads of baggage." And Greene wrote to Governor Cooke of Rhode Island: ". . . the Lord seems to have smote the enemy with panic." The elation spread to Philadelphia. To the account of the battles which Robert Morris sent to Deane he added that "these feats have turned the scale," that the militia were turning out in Maryland, New Jersey, and Pennsylvania, and that the same was reported from Rhode Island.

Hackensack, Newark, and Elizabeth Town, together with many prisoners and much baggage, were taken by the patriot forces. Within a few days they occupied the shore opposite Staten Island, and the American lines stretched all the way to Woodbridge. The light horse captured a wagon train laden with woollen clothing, which was invaluable to the ragged American soldiers. In Monmouth County a party of fifty Waldeckers surrendered after losing eight or ten of their number in a fight with local minute-men.

So bright seemed the prospect that Washington appears to have intended to remain at Morristown only long enough to refresh his men. But a general must have soldiers in order to take advantage of even the best of opportunities, and by the 7th he was reporting to the Congress that although the enemy had evacuated Trenton and Princeton, they were concentrated at New Brunswick in great force, whereas in his own army, he wrote: "Every day more and more leave us."

Some, to be sure, retained their martial spirit. Moulder's gunners were cheered by the reappearance of their battery waiter, whom they had last seen at Princeton, and who now turned up with a cart loaded with poultry. When Washington asked them to stay on for three weeks after the expiration of their enlistments until the arrival of the newly raised regiments, they assured him that they would stay, in his service, three weeks, three months, or three years. But some of the other Pennsylvania militia were less willing. They had suffered greatly from the lack of their blankets, which they had not seen again until the baggage train made the long journey from Burlington, and they had already, as Washington admitted, undergone more fatigue and hardship than he expected of militia.

Morristown was a pleasant village consisting of some fifty houses, a church, and Freeman's Tavern, at which Washington set up his headquarters. There was plenty of timber in the neighborhood, and the soldiers built cabins which, after the hardships of the past two months, seemed quite comfortable. Supplies were to be had from the surrounding country. But most of the time-expired men—miserable, bored, and homesick as they were—could by no means be prevailed upon to remain with the colors. Some Maryland militia and a troop of Virginia light horse joined the army. Before very long the first of the new regiments began to arrive. But the weather continued to be bitterly cold. A great many of the men were still ill clad and shoeless. For the captures of clothing and footgear were altogether inadequate to supply their wants. Smallpox appeared among the troops. There was a deplorable amount of drinking, swearing, fighting, and stealing. Some of the excellent horses captured at Princeton were not delivered up to the proper authorities, and Washington was compelled to issue an order promising dire punishment for those found guilty of concealing them.

Morristown, however, turned out to be one of the best possible places in which to pass this time of military impotence. So long as Washington remained there, with even the skeleton of an army, his presence constituted a threat to the flank of any attempt by the British to renew their advance on Philadelphia. The mountain barrier that stretches from Pluckemin almost to the Passaic screened his position, and the roads leading from it to the Delaware and the Hudson, from observation by the enemy on the plain below. The village itself was highly defensible. Situated on a lofty triangular plateau, with Thimble Mountain behind it and steep slopes on the other two sides, it could be approached only by rugged defiles of such natural strength that the

British shrank from the losses that would be incurred in forcing them.

With his nest egg of an army thus secure, Washington turned this period of enforced inactivity to excellent account. In a statesmanlike effort to win the support of the tories—so many of whom had been alienated from their old loyalty by the treatment they had received from the British and Hessian soldiery—Washington had caused to be posted "in the most public parts of the Jerseys" a proclamation, dated January 1st, in which all troops under his command were forbidden to plunder "any person whatsoever, whether tories or others." "The effects of such persons," it was stated, "will be applied to public uses in a regular manner, and it is expected that humanity and tenderness to women and children will distinguish brave Americans, contending for liberty, from infamous mercenary ravagers, whether British or Hessians."

This he followed on January 9th with another proclamation. In the latter, making full use of his authority as dictator, he strictly commanded all persons who had been deluded by the Howes' promise of pardon and protection into taking oaths of allegiance to the King "to repair to Headquarters or to the quarters of the nearest general officer of the Continental Army or Militia . . . and take the oath of allegiance to the United States of America," or else to withdraw themselves and their families within the enemy lines. Those who did not follow either of these courses within the next thirty days would be "deemed adherents to the King of Great Britain and tried as common enemies of the American States."

But the lot of the tories in New Jersey was a hard

one this winter in spite of Washington's promise of amnesty. Certain of them had ridden roughshod over their patriot neighbors during the weeks of the British occupation. The depredations of British and Hessian troops and the retaliation of them by local irregulars had roused great bitterness on both sides. At Trenton on the evening of January 2nd an American army chaplain who had failed to make good his retreat across the Assanpink had been murdered in cold blood by British soldiers. Next morning a British officer who was riding from New Brunswick to rejoin his regiment at Princeton was shot from ambush by American guerrillas, who stripped his body and left it on the highway.

Now American soldiers on their way home from the army rejoiced to see parties of tories that numbered between twenty-six and forty marched into Burlington under guard and sent to row the galleys of Seymour's flotilla. Wagons were brought in laden with goods which the tories were charged with having looted from those who had supported the cause of Independence. In vain did the loyalists assert that the evidence of plundering at Trenton and Burlington had been manufactured for purposes of propaganda. They went to jail by the wagonload. The American troops, according to Stedman, were permitted to plunder only those who remained faithful to the King, but this they appear to have done, as he says, with "every barbarity," even "scourges and stripes."

But Washington's first care during that winter was, of course, the formation of a new army, and particularly for the improvement of the quality of its officers in the lower grades. Hitherto, as in the volunteer armies of the United States at the beginning of every war until 1917, the ranks had been full of intelligent self-sacrificing patriots, but the lieutenants and captains, and many of the majors and colonels, had too frequently been men whose chief qualification had been their ability as office-seekers. In October Greene had written to a friend: "We want nothing but good officers to constitute as good an army as ever marched into the field. Our men are infinitely better than the officers." On the 9th of January Washington instructed Colonel Baylor to "take none but gentlemen" as officers for a new cavalry regiment, adding that there had been no instance of good or bad behavior in his army that had not originated with the officers.

Washington's dictatorial powers authorized him to raise sixteen additional battalions of infantry, three thousand light horse, three regiments of artillery, and a corps of engineers. The new term of enlistment was three years. The battalions were to be raised from all the states indiscriminately, and he strove to discourage local feeling in the army by urging the substitution of "American"—"the greater name," as he said—for local designations. Large numbers of recruits came in on the new terms, though they came slowly, and when he marched nine or ten thousand of his troops through Philadelphia in the following summer, it was observed that, although they were indifferently dressed, their arms were well burnished and they carried themselves like soldiers.

Meanwhile he seized every opportunity—and of these there were many—to make life burdensome for the great garrisons at Perth Amboy and New Brunswick. "With his usual sagacity," as Stedman observes, Washington strove to keep his men from despondency

[133]

by continually "insulting, surprising, and cutting off pickets, advance guards, convoys, and foraging parties." This was the kind of fighting that came naturally to them, and they were like so many thorns in the British flesh.

· T H R E E ·

To the British troops who were crowded into the inadequate quarters available at New Brunswick and Perth Amboy, however, it seemed that the entire population of the state had turned against them. Their life was uncomfortable, dull, and dangerous. Putnam, who had somewhat tardily obeyed Washington's order to move his command to Princeton, kept mounted men in the dress of farmers patroling every country road; patriot spies catered for the British messes with calculated inefficiency; and the American troops at Woodbridge were only three miles away from Perth Amboy. No detachment of any sort could move out from either Perth Amboy or New Brunswick without its departure, and generally its mission, being speedily made known to vigilant and active enemies.

Fuel, food, and fodder had all to be sent from New York. Nothing could be got locally without fighting for it. Clinton's aide in New York wrote to him at Newport that there were "daily skirmishes in the Jerseys." Officers' messes were reduced to salt meat and ammunition bread, the latter so notorious that even the King had heard of it and deplored its badness. As evidence of the scarcity within the British lines, American soldiers observed with satisfaction the poor condition of the horses which they captured. "Amboy and Brunswick," Stedman writes, "were in a manner besieged."

In these circumstances the British garrisons in New Jersey felt none of the complacency of their commander-in-chief. To them the cold facts of the recent campaign were too obvious. Howe had had nearly twenty-three thousand of the best troops in the world at his disposal in the Jerseys, in New York, and on Staten Island. Washington had never been able to take the field against him with more than five thousand men; and those, by any formal military standard, had been ill armed and of the poorest quality. The men and officers killed on both sides since Christmas night numbered less than two hundred. Yet in a fortnight a whole province had been lost, save for the strongholds at New Brunswick and Perth Amboy and the post at Paulus Hook. And the two former were now suffering such continual and costly harassment that, in Stedman's opinion, a successful attack on Washington at Morristown could have been made with smaller loss. It is little wonder that Stedman added: "In all these transactions there was something inexplicable."

John Adams gave one good explanation. The Jersey people, he wrote to his wife on February 17th, "are actuated by resentment now; and resentment coinciding with principle is a very powerful motive." Another potent cause was the enormous gain in Washington's reputation, not only in New Jersey but throughout the country. As he had assumed sole responsibility for all that had gone wrong in the past, so now the recent successes were attributed solely to him. Patriots, tories, and neutrals were united in their pride in him as a fellow American. The growth of his authority and influence was correspondingly great, and his firm and temperate use of the extraordinary powers lately conferred upon him solidified the public confidence in him.

In England, too, it was not long before the true significance of the campaign was well understood both by the government and by all intelligent observers. Near the end of February Lord North was writing to the under-secretary of state for America to caution him against printing the account of Mawhood's action and Cornwallis's "march and retreat" in the all too truthful form in which it had been sent to him. A week earlier Horace Walpole had written to a friend: "the Court denies being certain of the discomfiture of the Hessians." But on the 27th he wrote: "The capture of the Hessians is confirmed, with circumstances somewhat untoward, for they were not surprised, and yet all laid down their arms. . . . It is now the fashion to cry up the manoeuvre of General Washington, who has beaten two British regiments, too, and obliged General Howe to contract his quarters—in short the campaign had been by no means wound up to content."

On March 5th he added: "The campaign in America has lost a great deal of its florid complexion, and General Washington is allowed by both sides not to be the worst general in the field." Three weeks later he was commenting on the Spartan fare which the increasing animosity of the neighboring population was inflicting on the garrison of New York, and on April 4th he told Sir Horace Mann that Washington had shown himself to be both a Fabius and a Camillus, and that his march from Trenton was acknowledged to be a masterpiece of strategy. Similar information, moreover, was available not only to such persons as Walpole but to all who read the London newspapers.

There appears to be no truth in the old legend that Frederick the Great expressed unbounded admiration for Washington's generalship at this time and sent him a sword. But the campaign that culminated at Princeton established Washington's reputation as a skillful and daring strategist in every army in Europe and at every court from the Kremlin to that of Madrid. Something of its effect on the entire course of the war began to be understood even by King George's ministers.

On March 3rd Germain wrote to the Howes in their capacity of His Majesty's Commissioners for restoring peace: "I trust . . . that the unexpected success of the rebels will not so far elate them as to prevent them from seeing the real horrors of their situation, and tempt them to disdain to sue for pardon." But that was precisely what it had done. In the four years that followed, Philadelphia was taken, an army starved and froze at Valley Forge, Savannah was lost, Charleston fell, the South was overrun, and patriots shuddered at the treason of Benedict Arnold. But never again were the hopes of American Independence to fall so low as the point from which Washington and his men raised them in the nine days between Christmas night, 1776, and the 4th of January, 1777.

BIBLIOGRAPHY

Albion, Robert Greenhalgh: *Introduction to Military History*, New York, 1929.

Albion, Robert Greenhalgh & Jennie Barnes Pope: *Sea Lanes in Wartime*, New York, 1942.

American Archives, 5th Series, Vol. III, Washington, 1853.

Barnsley, Edward R.: *Snap Shots of Revolutionary Newtown*, Vol. 8. Bucks County Historical Society Papers, Doylestown, Pennsylvania, 1940.

Belcher, Rev. Henry: *The First American Civil War*, Vol. I, London, 1911.

Brief Narrative of the Ravages of the British and Hessians at Princeton in 1776-77, Varnum Lansing Collins, ed., Princeton, New Jersey, 1906.

The Sir Henry Clinton Papers, at the Clements Memorial Library, University of Michigan, Ann Arbor, Michigan.

Curtis, Edward E., Ph.D.: *The British Army in the American Revolution*, New Haven, 1926.

Custis, George Washington Parke: *Memoirs of Washington*, New York, 1859.

Dictionary of American Biography, New York, 1935.

Dictionary of National Biography, New York, 1885.

Drake, Francis S.: *Life and Correspondence of Henry Knox, Major General in the American Revolutionary Army*, Boston, 1873.

Dunlap, William: *A History of the American Theatre*, New York, 1832.

Encyclopaedia Britannica, 11th Edition, New York, 1911.

Fiske, John: *The American Revolution*, Boston & New York, 1902.

Ford, Paul Leicester: *The True George Washington*, Philadelphia, 1897.

Ford, Worthington Chauncey: *The Writings of Washington*, New York & London, 1890.

Lord George Germain Papers, at the Clements Memorial Library, University of Michigan, Ann Arbor, Michigan.

[138]

Glyn, Ensign Thomas: *Ensign Thomas Glyn's Journal*, manuscript in Princeton University Library.

Greene, Francis Vinton: *The Revolutionary War & the Military Policy of the United States*, New York, 1911.

Greene, George Washington: *Life of Nathanael Greene, Major-General in the Army of the Revolution*, New York, 1871.

Haven, C. C.: *Thirty Days in New Jersey*, Trenton, 1867.

Hudleston, F. J.: *Gentleman Johnny Burgoyne*, New York, 1927.

———, *Warriors in Undress*, Boston, 1926.

Hughes, Rupert: *George Washington, Savior of the States, 1777-1781*, New York, 1930.

Hunter, Andrew: *Manuscript Diary of Andrew Hunter, Princeton Class of 1772, Chaplain of the New Jersey Brigade*, in Princeton University Library.

Irving, Washington, *Life of George Washington*, New York, 1855.

Jones, Judge Thomas: *History of New York during the Revolutionary War*, New York, 1879.

The William Knox Papers, at the Clements Memorial Library, University of Michigan, Ann Arbor, Michigan.

Letters from Major Baurmeister to Colonel von Junkenn, written during the Philadelphia Campaign, 1777-1778, edited by Bernard A. Uhlendorf & Edna Vosper, Philadelphia, 1937.

Lossing, Benson J.: *Pictorial Field Book of the Revolution*, New York, 1852.

Lowell, Edward J.: *The Hessians and Other German Auxiliaries of Great Britain in the Revolutionary War*, New York, 1884.

Maurice, Maj. Gen. Sir Frederick: *The History of the Scots Guards*, London, 1934.

McMunn, Lieut. Gen. Sir George, *The American War of Independence in Perspective*, London, 1939.

New York Gazette and Weekly Mercury, The, Dec. & Jan., 1776-1777.

Partridge, Bellamy: *Sir Billy Howe*, London, New York, Toronto, 1932.

Pearson, Hasketh: *Tom Paine, Friend of Mankind*, New York, 1937.

[139]

Pennsylvania Archives, 1760-76, Vol. 4, Philadelphia, 1853.

Rush, Benjamin, M.D.: *A Memorial, 1745-1813,* Philadelphia, 1905.

———, *Directions for Preserving the Health of Soldiers,* Lancaster (Pa.), 1777.

Sergeant R.'s Account of the Battle of Princeton, manuscript in the Princeton University Library.

Serle, Ambrose: *The American Journal of Ambrose Serle, Secretary to Lord Howe, 1776-1778,* E. H. Tatum, ed., Huntington Library, San Marino, California, 1940.

Sparks Manuscript, in Princeton University Library.

Sparks, Jared, ed.: *The Writings of George Washington,* Boston, 1834.

Stedman, Charles: *History of the Origin, Progress, and Termination of the American War,* London, 1794.

Stevens, B. F.: *Facsimiles of Manuscripts in European Archives Relating to America,* London, 1890.

Stiles, Ezra: *The Literary Diary of Ezra Stiles, D.D., LL.D.,* Franklin Bowditch Dexter, M.A., ed., New York, 1901.

Stokes, I. N. Phelps: *The Iconography of Manhattan Island,* Vol. V., New York, 1926.

Stryker, William S.: *The Battles of Trenton and Princeton,* Boston & New York, 1898.

Trevelyan, Rt. Hon. Sir George Otto, Bart.: *The American Revolution,* London, New York & Bombay, 1903.

Trumbull, John: *Autobiography, Reminiscences and Letters of John Trumbull,* New York & London, 1841.

Walpole, Horace: *Letters of Horace Walpole,* Mrs. Paget Toynbee, ed., Oxford, 1904.

Ward, Christopher L.: *The Delaware Continentals, 1776-1783,* Wilmington, Delaware, 1941.

Waterman, Joseph M.: *With Sword and Lancet, the Life of General Hugh Mercer,* Richmond, 1941.

Wertenbaker, Thomas Jefferson: *"The Battle of Princeton,"* in *The Princeton Battle Monument,* Princeton, 1922.

Wilkinson, Gen. James: *Memoirs of My Own Times,* Philadelphia, 1816.

INDEX

Adams, John, 16, 135
Albany, N.Y., 64
Allentown, N.J., 73, 77
Anderson, Captain R. C., 51
Armstrong, General John, 12
Arnold, General Benedict, 24, 25
Assanpink Creek, 27, 52, 54, 56, 95

Bacon, Francis, 68
Baldwin farm (now Prospect), 96
Baltimore, Md., 3, 24
Barnes, Major, house of, 82
Basking Ridge, N.J., 23
Battery, The, New York City, 64
Battle of Brooklyn, The, A Farce in Two Acts, 70
Baylor, Lieutenant Colonel George, 133
Beaumont, Doctor, British Surgeon General, 70
Bethlehem, Pa., 44
Birmingham, N.J., 49
Black Horse, N.J., 5, 36, 37
Bordentown, N.J., 5, 15, 16, 27, 35, 36, 72, 73, 77, 81
Boston, Mass., 3
Brief Narration, A ("The Olden Diary"), 103, 110
Bristol, Pa., 15, 27, 61
British Army, Discipline in, 31-32, 34, 66-68
Bülow, D. H. von, 121
Burgoyne, General Sir John, 20, 64
Burke, Edmund, 63
Burlington, N.J., 5, 15, 16, 35, 37, 76, 93, 132
Burns, Robert, 69

Cadwalader, General John, 12, 27, 61, 62, 75-77, 82, 94, 107, 109
Canada, 20, 64
"Canvass Town," 66
Carleton, Sir Guy, 22
Charleston, S.C., 3, 21, 67

Clark, Thomas, house of, 96, 97, 106, 114
Clark, William, house of, 105, 114
Clinton, General George, 19
Clinton, General Sir Henry, 3, 21, 25, 63, 64, 66
Commissioners, British, for restoring peace, 137
Committee of Three, Congressional, 4
Common Sense, pamphlet, 10, 70
Connecticut troops, 26, 45
Continental Congress, 3, 70, 79-80
Continental currency, 26, 76, 78
Cooke, Governor Nicholas, 128
Cooper's Creek, N.J., 37
Cornwallis, General Lord, 7, 9, 10, 16, 22, 34, 64, 81, 84, 85, 86, 88-89, 116, 117, 121, 123, 124, 136
Coryell's Ferry (New Hope, Pa.), 15
Cranbury, N.J., 74, 77
Crosswicks, N.J., 16, 82, 127

Deane, Silas, 116, 128
Dechow, Major Friedrich Ludwig von, 43, 44, 53, 54, 56, 58
Delancy, Captain Oliver, 70
Delaware troops, 10, 11, 45, 49, 97, 106
Dickinson, General Philemon, house of, 52
Donop, Colonel Carl Emil Kurt von, 35, 36-37, 59, 72, 73, 74-75, 81
Douglas, Alexander, house of, 90
Dunk's Ferry, 15
Durham boats, 28

Easton, Pa., 22, 24
Elizabeth Town, N.J., 32, 128
England, Opinion in, 63, 136-137
Erskine, Sir William, 88
Ewing, General James, 27, 61